PETER FLANNERY

Peter was writer in residence ~~~~~~ ~~~~ ᴐhakespeare
Company in 1979-1980. His plays first staged by the RSC
include *Singer*, which originally starred Antony Sher, and won
the Time Out Best Play Award in 1989, and was subsequently
revived by the Oxford Stage Company in 2004, starring Ron
Cook; *Our Friends in the North*, winner of the 1982 John
Whiting Award; *Savage Amusement*, which won the Best Play
Award at the National Student Drama Festival, 1978. Other
theatre includes *The Bodies*, adapted from Émile Zola's *Thérèse
Raquin* for Live Theatre, Newcastle, in 2005.

Television and film work includes *The Devil's Whore* (Channel
4, 2008); *George Gently*, adapted from the novels by Alan
Hunter (BBC One, 2007); *The One and Only* (Pathé, 2003);
Our Friends in the North (BBC Two, 1996), based on his
original stage play, winner of the Writers' Guild Award for Best
Original Drama Serial, the Broadcasting Press Guild Award for
Writer of the Year, the BAFTA for Best Drama Serial and the
Royal Television Society Writers' Award; *Funny Bones* with
Peter Chelsom (Hollywood Pictures, 1995); *Shoot the
Revolution* (BBC Two, 1990); and *Blind Justice* (BBC Two,
1988), winner of the Royal Television Society Award for Best
Series and the Samuel Beckett Award. Peter also won the
BAFTA Dennis Potter Award in 1996.

Peter Flannery

BURNT BY THE SUN

after the screenplay by
Nikita Mikhalkov and Rustam Ibragimbekov

NICK HERN BOOKS

London

www.nickhernbooks.co.uk

A Nick Hern Book

This adaptation of *Burnt by the Sun* first published in Great Britain as a paperback original in 2009 by Nick Hern Books Limited, 14 Larden Road, London W3 7ST

This adaptation of *Burnt by the Sun* copyright © 2009 Peter Flannery
Original screenplay © 1994 Nikita Mikhalkov and Rustam Ibragimbekov

Peter Flannery has asserted his right to be identified as the author of this work

Cover image: Girl at Young Pioneer Camp, Khabarovsk, USSR in 1966.
© Dean Conger/CORBIS
Cover design: Ned Hoste, 2H

Typeset by Nick Hern Books, London
Printed and bound in Great Britain by CPI Bookmarque, Croydon, Surrey

A CIP catalogue record for this book is available from the British Library

ISBN   978 1 84842 044 1

Mixed Sources
Product group from well-managed forests and other controlled sources
www.fsc.org Cert no. TT-COC-002227
© 1996 Forest Stewardship Council
FSC

Burnt by the Sun was first performed in the Lyttelton
auditorium of the National Theatre, London, on 3 March 2009
(previews from 24 February), with the following cast:

NADIA	Skye Bennett / Holly Gibbs
MAROUSSIA	Michelle Dockery
KOTOV	Ciaran Hinds
LIDIA	Rowena Cooper
ELENA	Anna Carteret
MOKHOVA	Stephanie Jacob
VSEVOLOD	Duncan Bell
OLGA	Pamela Merrick
LITTLE GIRLS	Anna Burnett / Floss Hoffman / Hattie Webb
KOLYA	Stuart Martin
ANDRUSHYA	Michael Grady-Hall
KIRIK	Tim McMullan
TRUCK DRIVER	Tony Turner
MITIA	Rory Kinnear
BLOKHIN	Roger Ringrose
MIRONOV	Colin Haigh
ARONIN	Margus Cunningham
PIONEER OFFICERS	Michael Grady-Hall, Harry Hepple, Stuart Martin
ENSEMBLE	Anne Kavanagh, Victoria Lennox, Charlotte Pyke

Director   Howard Davies
Designer   Vicki Mortimer
Lighting Designer   Mark Henderson
Music   Ilona Sekacz
Choreographer   Scarlett Mackmin
Sound Designer   Christopher Shutt
Music Director   Dan Jackson

Characters

NADIA, *nearly ten*
MAROUSSIA, *twenty-nine, Nadia's mother*
KOTOV, *fifty, Maroussia's husband*
LIDIA, *seventy, Maroussia's grandmother*
ELENA, *seventy, Lidia's friend*
MOKHOVA, *forty, the maid*
VSEVOLOD, *fifty, Lidia's son*
OLGA, *fifty, Maroussia's mother, Vselvolod's sister-in-law*
KOLYA, *twenties, a tank officer*
ANDRUSHYA, *twenties, a tank officer*
KIRIK, *forty, Elena's son*
TRUCK DRIVER
MITIA, *thirty-six*
BLOKHIN, *an NKVD officer*
MIRONOV, *an NKVD officer*
ARONIN, *an NKVD officer*

Also a VOCALIST, MUSICIANS, *two little* GIRLS, *a band of* YOUNG PIONEERS *and their* ADULT OFFICERS.

The action takes place in Nikolina Gora, a village twenty-two miles west of Moscow, from 1936

This text went to press before the end of rehearsals and so may differ slightly from the play as performed.

ACT ONE

Scene One

1936. Early morning on a summer's day. A dacha near Moscow.
There is no sign of life in the house, nor in the garden, nor on the
verandah. All we can see in the house is a large music room in
which sits a grand piano with a double stool. The walls are hung
with framed photographs and are otherwise lined with books.
There is also a small table with a wind-up gramophone on it. On
the verandah is a large circular dining table and enough chairs
for eight. There is also a rocking chair. The verandah has a low
balustrade separating it from the garden and some wooden steps
leading down. The verandah and the music room are linked by
French windows, which are permanently open.

Enter four MUSICIANS *into the garden – guitar, accordion,*
violin and vocalist. They are dressed in white suits. They
arrange themselves before the house and get ready to play in
tune. The VOCALIST *gives them the time under his breath, and*
with a hand movement.

VOCALIST. One, two, three, four…

> *They strike up an Argentinian tango called 'The Weary Sun'.*
> *After a few bars, a bedroom window – upstage of the music*
> *room – flies open and* NADIA *climbs out in her nightdress*
> *and stands, enraptured at the sight and sound of the*
> MUSICIANS. *She shouts as loud as she can.*

NADIA. Mamma! Pappa! They're here! The holiday's started!
Long life to Comrade Stalin's balloons and airships!!

> *She beams at them as the* VOCALIST *begins to sing.*

VOCALIST (*singing*).
> Burnt by the sun,
> As the crimson sea did run,

I heard you say, my dove,
That there would be no love.

NADIA's mother MAROUSSIA comes out, via the verandah, also in her nightdress. She stands with NADIA and smiles at them and at her.

Her husband KOTOV comes out, naked to the waist, his arms tattooed.

(*Singing*.)
Let's leave one another now –
I won't hold it against you…

After a while, MAROUSSIA leads KOTOV into the garden and they start to dance a tango. NADIA watches, picks up the steps, joins them in the garden and dances her own tango.

MAROUSSIA's grandmother LIDIA and her friend ELENA emerge in dressing gowns and slippers. They watch and then dance together on the verandah.

MOKHOVA, in her maid's uniform, comes out and takes in the scene. She disappears for a while and comes back with breakfast settings. She sets the table on the verandah, having to work around the GRANNIES as they dance. LIDIA's son VSEVOLOD and his sister-in-law OLGA come out in dressing gowns. They start to dance in the garden.

NADIA. Mokhova! Mokhova?! Come and dance!

MOKHOVA joins her in the garden and they dance. After a while, VSEVOLOD engineers a swap of partners so that he has MOKHOVA and NADIA has her grandmother OLGA. MOKHOVA has to keep VSEVOLOD's hands from straying.

The song continues, but before it can reach its conclusion it is drowned out by the noise of low-flying aircraft right overhead.

The GRANNIES nearly die of fright.

NADIA *clings to her mother.*

MOKHOVA *screams.* VSEVOLOD *immediately clasps her to his bosom. She pulls herself free. He pinches her bottom, unseen in the confusion.*

Another aircraft screams overhead. And another. Only KOTOV *raises his arms to the skies and greets the planes with unsuppressed joy.*

KOTOV. Beautiful! Beautiful! Aren't they beautiful!?

VSEVOLOD (*disturbed*). What are they doing here?

MAROUSSIA (*to* KOTOV). The celebrations. Is it for the celebrations?

KOTOV holds his arms wide open. How should he know?

Two little GIRLS *run on, shouting.*

GIRL ONE. Nadia! Nadia! There are tanks in the wheat field! Get your father! Get Comrade Kotov!

She sees KOTOV *and comes to attention before him.*

GIRL TWO. Comrade Kotov! You have to come and save the wheat!

KOTOV. Me?

GIRL ONE. They told us to run as quick as we could to fetch you!

GIRL TWO. You have to come and save the wheat from the tanks!

KOTOV. Why me, little girl? Where are the men from the village? Where's the Chairman of the Co-operative?

GIRL ONE. He's hitting the tanks with his walking stick!

GIRL TWO. The old women are crying! Come quick! They're going to ride their tanks over the wheat!

KOTOV. It's my day off! It's a holiday!

NADIA. Pappa! Do as they ask! You have to save the wheat!

He grabs her and runs with her over his shoulder. She squeals with delight.

KOTOV. Oh, I have to, do I!? I have to do what bossy-boots Nadia tells me, do I?

Enter two tank officers, KOLYA and ANDRUSHYA, in no mood for delay or fun and games. Two more planes scream overhead. KOTOV raises his arms to them once more.

They're *so* beautiful!!

He could eat them up. KOLYA spots him.

KOLYA. Hey! You! With the big mouth! Which one of you is Kotov?

KOTOV points inquiringly to himself.

Yes, you! Are you the bag of wind the morons want us to talk to?

KOTOV (*to everybody*). Is he talking to me?

KOLYA. Are you the big cheese round here? What are you, the Chairman?

KOTOV. Me? No. But tell me, pretty boy, why are your tanks in the people's wheat field, eh? Whose bright idea was this, eh?

ANDRUSHYA (*admiring his nerve*). 'Bright idea'? Listen, old man, orders from above.

KOTOV. Ah. Orders from above. Who's in charge?

KOLYA. Never mind 'who's in charge', old timer. Just tell your friends to get out of the wheat field or I'll drive my tanks straight over them.

KOTOV. Ah. You'll drive your tanks straight over them, will you?

KOLYA. You heard.

KOTOV. Stand to attention!

KOLYA. Eh?

KOTOV. Stand to attention! Both of you!

They almost do so, so commanding is his voice and manner.

ANDRUSHYA. Who is he? Who do you think you are?

KOTOV. You don't know me?

KOLYA. No!

KOTOV. Comrade Lieutenant, tell your pretty-boy friend who I am.

ANDRUSHYA. I don't know who you are!

KOTOV. You don't know me either!?

ANDRUSHYA. No!

KOTOV. You don't know me!? I'll wipe my arse with you both!

He takes ANDRUSHYA*'s peaked cap and pulls it onto his own head. He turns his head so they see him in profile.*

Eh? Eh? Like this? Eh?

A stunned silence.

KOLYA. Is it… is it…?

KOTOV. Go on: say it!

It starts to dawn on them who he is.

ANDRUSHYA. Kotov…?

KOLYA. Kotov. Is it… *Comrade* Kotov?

KOTOV. Got me now, pretty boy?

ANDRUSHYA. Kotov…? General Kotov?

KOTOV. Excellent! Now: who's in charge?

But they can only smile like bashful girls in the presence of their hero.

KOLYA. It's Comrade Kotov…

KOTOV. I said, who's in charge?

KOLYA. You are.

ANDRUSHYA. You are. (*Then, realising the question, he points to* KOLYA.) Him.

KOLYA. Me. No. Brigadier Commander Lapin.

KOTOV. Oh, that idiot!

KOLYA*'s radio starts to crackle with an angry voice on the other end.* KOTOV *seizes it and barks into it.*

Who am I talking to here? Speak up!

ANDRUSHYA (*to* KOLYA). It's General Kotov.

KOTOV. Pull yourselves together.

KOTOV *can't hear the voice clearly. He bangs the radio on the balustrade. We hear a howl of pain on the other end.*

(*About the clarity on the line.*) That's better. Micha, how are you? Eh? Why aren't I advancing? Because it's the people who plant the wheat, Micha, not you, so what are your tanks doing in their wheat field? Explain. Explain or I'll be dialling Moscow 2315. Know whose private line that is? Comrade Stalin! 'Who's this talking?' Don't you remember me, Micha? It's Serguei! Tell him.

He hands the radio to KOLYA.

KOLYA (*shouting with excitement*). It's Kotov!

ANDRUSHYA. It's Kotov!

Silence on the radio. Then a burst of excited babble.

KOLYA (*to* KOTOV). He says, 'What are your orders, sir?'

A burst of applause, led by NADIA.

KOTOV. That's better! Tell him I want you to take your beautiful tanks…

KOLYA (*into radio*). He wants us to take our beautiful tanks…

KOTOV. And your beautiful planes…

KOLYA (*into radio*). And our beautiful planes…

KOTOV. And piss off with them.

    A beat.

KOLYA (*into radio*). And go away.

KOTOV. Please.

KOLYA (*into radio*). Please.

KOTOV. And thank you.

    He listens and hangs up.

KOLYA. He says, 'Yes, sir.'

    Cheering and celebrations. KOTOV *looks at the* GIRLS *and points offstage. The* GIRLS *run off. Even* ANDRUSHYA *and* KOLYA *are grinning from ear to ear.*

    I knew him straight away. Comrade Kotov.

ANDRUSHYA. I'd've spotted him straight away if he'd been on his horse…

MAROUSSIA (*mischievously*). My apologies for my husband. He was rude to you. He'll say sorry.

KOTOV. Rude…?

MAROUSSIA. And coarse.

KOLYA. No, no, no…

KOTOV. Me? Coarse?

MAROUSSIA. You said you'd wipe your… bottom… with them.

KOTOV. I said that?

ANDRUSHYA. No. No, no…

KOTOV. Nadia. Was I rude to the Comrade Lieutenants…?

    A beat.

NADIA. I didn't hear anything.

Laughter. He swings her onto his shoulders and puts his arm around MAROUSSIA*'s waist.*

The band strikes up the same tune again, softly.

MOKHOVA. Breakfast! Breakfast is ready!

KOTOV *stands to attention and salutes* KOLYA *and* ANDRUSHYA. *So does* NADIA, *from on high. So does* MAROUSSIA, *smiling warmly at them.*

KOTOV. What's your name?

KOLYA. Kotov. Kolya.

KOTOV. Kolya. Go and do your duty for our beloved motherland. A soldier must always carry out his orders. But remember, Kolya, who it is that puts the food in our mouths... Yes? Dismiss.

They nod. A lesson learnt. They salute once more, turn on their heels and march off.

The MUSICIANS *are leaving, playing as they go.* NADIA *is waving to them.*

NADIA. See you later at the celebrations for Comrade Stalin's airships and balloons!

They wave to her and are nearly gone, the tune lingering a while. The planes roar past, overhead, leaving as they came.

KOTOV. There they go. Beautiful...

MAROUSSIA *puts her hand on his face, tenderly.*

MAROUSSIA. I'm not ready for breakfast. Let's go to the steam hut.

NADIA. Hurrah! The steam hut!

KOTOV *kisses* MAROUSSIA. *They leave, going around the house, as the others are pouring tea and settling at the breakfast table.*

Scene Two

Later. VSEVOLOD *is draining the dregs of the tea and reading yesterday's* Pravda.

MOKHOVA *has lost something important and is searching the verandah and garden for it, without wanting to attract attention.* VSEVOLOD *watches her any time she bends over. He makes her squeeze past him. He pinches her bottom.*

OLGA *is still in her dressing gown, but is now drying her hair in a towel.* LIDIA *is sipping tea in her dressing gown.*

OLGA. Why do they have to go to that little steam hut, eh? Can anybody tell me?

VSEVOLOD. Mm...?

He's secretly watching MOKHOVA, *who is on her hands and knees in the garden, bottom in the air.*

OLGA. Vsevolod? I'm asking...

VSEVOLOD. Mm...?

OLGA. What are you looking at?

VSEVOLOD. Yesterday's *Pravda*.

ELENA *enters in a dressing gown and unfinished fur coat.*

LIDIA. Ah!

LIDIA *applauds* ELENA *quietly as she does a twirl to show off the coat.*

ELENA. It's not finished.

OLGA. What I'm saying is: why does Serguei Petrovich have to take his wife to a barbaric little steam hut when we have a nice bathroom here...? Does anybody know? Elena, you're wearing a fur coat.

ELENA. It isn't finished.

OLGA. In the summer?

VSEVOLOD. Pushkin used a steam hut…

OLGA (*jumping in*). Yes, Pushkin used a steam hut – but did he take a ten-year-old girl in there with him? I doubt it. What would Boris Konstantinovich have said if he knew our daughter would marry the sort of man who prefers a steam hut to a bathroom?

A beat.

VSEVOLOD. I don't know.

Enter KOTOV *with some unopened letters. He's in a linen suit, shirt and tie. He doesn't sit at the table. He sits in his rocking chair, separate, where he leafs through the mail.*

ELENA. Vsevolod, what do you think? It's not finished. Lidia Stepanovna is making it with me.

VSEVOLOD *is miles away, staring at* MOKHOVA's *haunches.*

KOTOV. You're wasting your time, Elena. Vsevolod's like Switzerland. Well-fed and apathetic.

VSEVOLOD. I'm not apathetic, Serguei Petrovich. I'm passionate, if you must know. And thirsty.

LIDIA. Yes, Mokhova, where is Vsevolod Konstantinovich's morning coffee? What have you lost?

She and ELENA *know the answer very well.*

MOKHOVA (*going*). Nothing. I have lost nothing.

ELENA. Then what are you looking for?

MOKHOVA. I'll get the coffee.

ELENA. What do you think of my coat? Olga, who would ever have thought… at my age… reduced to making my own coats…?

KOTOV *glances at her but says nothing.*

VSEVOLOD. Have you hidden Mokhova's potions again?

LIDIA. It can't be allowed to go on. She'll poison herself.

KOTOV. Who...?

ELENA. Mokhova. She's addicted to those quack medicines.

OLGA. She's going to kill herself.

VSEVOLOD. There's only one known cure for her ailment.

LIDIA. Someone said take iron so she boiled up a pan of nails and drank the water.

KOTOV *is reading letters, half-listening, chuckling.*

KOTOV. What ailment is that, Vsevolod Konstantinovich?

VSEVOLOD. Middle-aged virginity. That's what she's suffering from.

MOKHOVA *brings in coffee which she puts on the table. They pour coffee. She stands in silence.*

MOKHOVA. I cannot find my pills.

Silence. They drink.

My pills have gone. Again.

KOTOV *sighs at this tiresome rigmarole, but says nothing.* MAROUSSIA *comes in.*

MAROUSSIA. Where's Nadia?

ELENA (*twirling*). Maroussia. My coat? It's not finished.

MAROUSSIA *smiles her approval and applauds silently and briefly.*

KOTOV. She's watching from the window. The Pioneers are passing by. She can't wait to be old enough to join them.

LIDIA. I don't understand all these celebrations they have. One after the other. What's it for today?

ELENA. Ask Nadia. Only little Nadia knows all the Soviet celebrations.

MOKHOVA. Someone has taken all my pills, all my powders, and all my herbs.

MAROUSSIA. Mokhova, are you all right – are you sure you've looked...?

VSEVOLOD. She won't be all right until she gets the full treatment. Listen, Serguei Petrovich, in yesterday's *Pravda* it says... 'Confession is the source of all justice. And – '

OLGA. Vsevolod, ssh, please, none of us wants to hear all this.

VSEVOLOD. I'm just asking Serguei. Serguei? 'Confession is the source of all justice...'? That's what they're saying at these hearings in Moscow. The State Prosecutor himself. What do they mean by that?

Silence. MOKHOVA *starts to cry.*

KOTOV (*getting irritated*). You're the one who teaches law. Mokhova, stop crying and tell Nadia to come down for breakfast.

MOKHOVA *leaves.*

MAROUSSIA. What's happened to her pills?

VSEVOLOD. I thought evidence was the source of all justice. Or is that an old-fashioned idea nowadays? We still teach it at the university at any rate. I'll have to be careful.

MAROUSSIA (*to the* GRANNIES). Have you hidden them again? Grandmother, have you hidden – ?

VSEVOLOD. I was trying to say something important, Maroussia. There have been more purges at the law faculty. They've dismissed a lot of professors.

KOTOV. But not you, Vsevolod. For you, life sails serenely on...

MAROUSSIA. Where are her pills?

*KOTOV holds up his hand for silence. They hear
MOKHOVA howling in her bedroom.*

KOTOV. Now Mokhova is howling.

VSEVOLOD. Well, I thought it was an important question,
Serguei. A question a man like you might know the answer
to.

KOTOV. Why should I know the answer? Why don't we wait
for the evidence – ?

VSEVOLOD. My point. If Kamenev and Zinoviev have
confessed, will we ever hear any evidence? Don't you ever
feel like asking yourself what's happening these days?

A beat.

KOTOV. Have faith.

Silence.

VSEVOLOD. Faith. Of course. I can't... Yes, life is serene, of
course... in this madhouse.

*Silence. He doesn't just mean the dacha. They look at
KOTOV, who stares and goes back to his letters.*

MAROUSSIA. Mother? Where are her pills?

VSEVOLOD. Oh, for heaven's sake, Maroussia: Elena and
Lidia threw her pills into the river!

KOTOV (*quietly*). Vsevolod? Don't raise your voice to
Maroussia.

*MAROUSSIA leaves quickly, exasperated, as KIRIK rides
into the garden on his bicycle, saluting and ringing his bell.*

KIRIK. Hurrah! Happy holidays, Comrades!

*He parks his bike and runs onto the verandah, where he
kisses OLGA's hand flirtatiously. Then ELENA, on the
cheek. He puts a paper bag on the table: a gift.*

Biscuits! Olga. Not dressed…? Hello, Mother. Why is Mokhova howling again?

He helps himself to coffee.

VSEVOLOD. Why do you think, Kirik? We all know what she needs.

KIRIK. Yes! Music!

He takes a disc from his shoulder bag and goes inside. Soon we hear an elegaic opera duet playing indoors.

KIRIK *comes back and stands with his coffee. He senses the silence around the table.*

KOTOV. Drinking coffee, Kirik?

KIRIK. Of course.

KOTOV. What – too early in the day for vodka?

ELENA. Serguei, you know Kirik doesn't drink alcohol any more. Never a drop.

Nobody else believes this.

KOTOV. Uh-huh?

ELENA. He made his mother a promise. A solemn promise.

KIRIK *blows her a long kiss. They all listen to the music. Some humming under their breath.*

KIRIK. Serguei Petrovich, you really shouldn't think of drinking as a vice anyway.

KOTOV. No?

KIRIK. No… it's the… what is it…?

He looks to OLGA *for help.*

The balm of the…?

OLGA. The balm of the tormented soul.

KIRIK. 'Tormented soul.' Exactly, my love!

VSEVOLOD. Tormented soul, eh? Mm. How exactly is your soul being tormented? Existential loneliness?

KIRIK. Vsevolod Konstantinovich, you remind me of Trofimov in Chekhov.

VSEVOLOD. Ah. *Cherry Orchard*.

KIRIK. You and all your friends at the university. Eternal students.

VSEVOLOD. Oh, no. They aren't my friends.

He glances at KOTOV, *who looks at him.*

'My friends...' as Pushkin says, 'My friends are no more or far away...' And which of us can truly say any different...?

The music has ended. They sit in silence. MAROUSSIA *comes in and sits with coffee.*

MAROUSSIA. I've calmed her down. I've promised her she can come with us to the zoo.

LIDIA. The zoo. Again.

MAROUSSIA. Nadia loves the zoo.

OLGA. Maroussia. When I was your age we never bothered with zoos and the like; we had the opera twice a week. Do you remember? Twice a week we saw great ballets and wonderful concerts. Remember, Maroussia?

MAROUSSIA. I was little, Mother.

OLGA (*important to her*). But you can remember...?

MAROUSSIA *doesn't reply. She sips her coffee.*

LIDIA. Ah, what days...

VSEVOLOD. What nights. Life was... full.

ELENA. And sweet... The chamber music we used to hear in this very house... before...

She glances nervously at KOTOV *who appears to be reading letters.*

Well... before...

*They relax into the quiet pleasure of nostalgic memories.
Silence. KOTOV gets up quickly. MAROUSSIA tries to
deter him from what she knows is coming.*

MAROUSSIA. Serguei...

KOTOV. No, no, Marousse, don't worry... It was a good life
you all had. No, really, I enjoy hearing you reminisce about
'before'. Which is just as well...

They chuckle.

But, you know, one question comes into my mind over and
over when I hear you talking about that good life you used to
enjoy so much.

MAROUSSIA (*gently*). Serguei...?

KOTOV. It's a question worth asking, Maroussia. (*A pause.*)
Why didn't you defend it?

He leaves a silence. They wait.

Why didn't you defend it? Mm? If it meant so much – if the
loss of it blights your lives... 'Oh, the old days... oh, for the
old days...' Then why didn't you lift a finger to defend what
you had?

Vsevolod Konstantinovich, why? Tell me. You – the
intelligentsia, with all your culture, your Italian opera, your
French books, your William Shakespeare, your two thousand
years of art and literature that meant the world to you. Why?
Why did you run away from a bunch of semi-literate
Bolsheviks like me? Mm? Why didn't you fight?

LIDIA. What do you mean, Serguei? What are you saying?

OLGA. Who's your husband angry with, Maroussia? Is it me? I
was only reminding Maroussia –

KOTOV (*walking round the table*). I'm not angry. I'm just
asking him.

VSEVOLOD. I don't know what you mean.

KOTOV. Why didn't you defend it?

VSEVOLOD. We did defend it.

KOTOV. You defended it? You ran away.

VSEVOLOD. Who?

KOTOV. You did. Why? Why did you run away? You were armed, you were clever... Why run away from ignorant peasants like me with our arses hanging out of our pants?

VSEVOLOD. We weren't soldiers.

KOTOV. Was I a soldier? Was I born with a gun in my hand? You think they taught me warfare in the shed I had my school days in? No. Nobody taught me to fight. Never. I learnt. I learnt because that was my choice. And I pursued you from the Urals to Siberia. Tracked you down. I fought for my life... And you... ran for yours.

Silence.

VSEVOLOD. Serguei Petrovich. Violence is a philosophical issue for me.

KOTOV. Of course. My dear scholar. It was a philosophical issue for you. As usual. And there's the answer to my question. You had nothing to offer, did you? Because all you wanted was for everything to stay the same. Nothing to change. And afterwards, why? After we changed everything? Why didn't you join the White Army and fight to overthrow us with your British and French friends? Because you thought we wouldn't last, didn't you? You thought it wouldn't last. But it has. So now you sit and remember the life you used to have. How happy you were listening to Puccini. While other people washed your clothes and fed you.

Silence. He sits in his chair. KIRIK *breaks the silence.*

KIRIK. Serguei Petrovich. I had flat feet.

They start to chuckle nervously, glad the mood might be broken.

You can mock me. I was wounded.

MAROUSSIA. Wounded...?

VSEVOLOD. Someone's husband found out and hit him with a billiard cue!

Laughter, even from KOTOV. *But the mood won't be dispelled.*

MAROUSSIA (*quietly*). Are you all right?

KOTOV. I'm fine, Maroussia, fine.

MOKHOVA *comes in and starts clearing the table in a huff. Silence.*

ELENA. I need a lie-down.

LIDIA. Me too. My head is spinning.

They toddle off. OLGA *gets up and goes. After a half-decent interval,* KIRIK *follows her. Finally* VSEVOLOD *folds his* Pravda *with dignity and leaves. Silence.* MAROUSSIA *looks at* KOTOV *and smiles sadly. She loves him, but she wishes this didn't happen. He spreads his arms as if to say 'What else am I supposed to do?'*

MAROUSSIA. All they have is the past.

She leaves with a gentle pat on his shoulder as she passes him. KOTOV *sits, watching* MOKHOVA. *Then he leaves.*

Scene Three

The sound of a car horn and an engine stopping. MOKHOVA *looks across the garden. Enter a* TRUCK DRIVER, *with a piece of paper in his hands.*

DRIVER. Hello? Excuse me? Hello? Is this... 'Zagorienka'...?

He's squinting at the paper.

MOKHOVA. Where?

DRIVER. Or 'Zagorienko'...? I washed my shirt with the delivery address in the pocket and now I can't read it.

He looks at MOKHOVA *properly and takes off his hat. He smiles.*

Hello.

She goes down into the garden.

MOKHOVA. Hello. I've never heard of Zagorienko.

DRIVER. Or Zagorienka...?

MOKHOVA. No.

DRIVER. Damn. I'm going round in circles. Who lives here? Who are all the kids on the road?

MOKHOVA. The Pioneers. For the celebrations.

DRIVER. What are we celebrating this time?

MOKHOVA. I don't know. I never understand the celebrations...

They chuckle. She's shy with him.

DRIVER. Well. The Pioneers are heading this way.

MOKHOVA. Yes. They'll go to the river. To practise their swimming. And their civil defence.

DRIVER. 'Civil defence'?

MOKHOVA. In case the Imperialist powers attack us with poison gas.

The sound of the Pioneer band approaching.

DRIVER. Yes. Well. I better get my truck out of their way. I'm trying to deliver some furniture. This isn't Zagorienka then...?

She shakes her head. He goes. He comes back and takes her hand. Silence between them.

NADIA *arrives from the house, running.*

NADIA. The Pioneers are coming!

She stands to attention and salutes. The DRIVER *kisses* MOKHOVA*'s hand and leaves.* MOKHOVA *stands for a second, looking at her hand.*

MOKHOVA. Oh. Oh...

She dashes inside.

Scene Four

The band of YOUNG PIONEERS *parades through the garden, playing flutes, trumpets, trombones and drums. They carry a big banner showing a picture of Stalin, and another – smaller – showing Kotov in characteristic profile with his peaked hat on. The same portrait of Kotov is on their tunics. This is the Kotov Brigade. They are singing a song in praise of Stalin.*

Bringing up the rear is a strange OLD MAN. *He has a long beard, long hair under a wide hat, dark glasses, a scruffy old raincoat and a white stick. He limps along, blowing tunelessly on a trumpet.*

The PIONEERS *do a circuit of the garden and start to leave.*

He limps along behind them, but as they disappear, he peels off and stands still, sniffing the air. NADIA *is worried about him. She drops her salute and stands behind the balustrade of the verandah. He goes on sniffing, apparently picking up a scent that starts to lead him towards her, tapping the ground with his stick.*

MITIA. What's that I can smell? No! It cannot be! Is it? Is it little Nadia, who's going to be a Pioneer and top of the class?

NADIA. How do you know that?

MITIA. Well… who wouldn't know the most brilliant little girl of them all?

NADIA. Are you the summer Santa?

MITIA. Yes, Nadia, I am the wizard from the Maghreb.

NADIA. Where's the Maghreb?

MITIA. It's the land where the summer Santas live.

NADIA. Is it in the USSR?

MITIA. Of course. All the summer Santas live in the USSR.

NADIA. And the winter ones?

MITIA. Them too.

She suddenly has a thought.

NADIA. Are you a doctor?

MITIA. A doctor? Probably.

NADIA. We need a doctor for Mokhova.

MITIA. Is she still here?

NADIA. Yes. Where else would Mokhova live?

MITIA. Got a husband yet?

NADIA. Who – Mokhova?

MITIA. Is she ill?

NADIA. No, but Great-Granny Lidia and Elena Mikhailovna
drowned all her medicine in the river. Then she howled like a
wolf.

MITIA. Are they still alive too? You better take me to
Mokhova.

*He holds out his hand, helplessly. She hesitates and then
takes it. She leads him inside the house. He starts singing an
aria from Puccini as she leads him.*

Scene Five

MOKHOVA *is dusting in the music room. She hears a voice
approaching which is singing Puccini. She looks up and sees
NADIA leading MITIA into the room. She screams.*

MOKHOVA. Who is this? Who let him in?

He gropes towards her, hands outstretched.

NADIA. He's a doctor, Mokhova. He's come to help you.

MITIA. I know your problem: you're still a virgin!

His hands touch her breasts. She screams again.

Away, white virgin!

OLGA *has arrived, very worried. She's fully dressed by now.*

OLGA. Who let this creature in?

He turns towards her voice.

MITIA. Ah! 'Lather makes Maroussia's skin so soft.'

OLGA. What? Why is he saying that?

VSEVOLOD *arrives and sees MITIA singing Puccini and
tapping his way around the room.*

VSEVOLOD. As if there weren't enough lunatics in this house! What do you want here?!

VSEVOLOD *bravery disappears as* MITIA *veers towards him.*

MITIA. Silence in court! We're hanging all the lawyers!

VSEVOLOD. What!? I demand you leave our house!

LIDIA *and* ELENA *have arrived, timidly.*

MITIA. Happy holidays, Grannies!

ELENA. I'm not a granny! Lidia?

LIDIA. Somebody help! Who let him in?

NADIA. I did. He's the summer Santa.

KIRIK *arrives, with* MAROUSSIA *not far behind.*

KIRIK. Leave the house immediately! Or else.

MITIA. Ah. He's here as well. The lover of strong drink… and weak women.

He starts towards KIRIK, *who takes evasive action. This brings* MITIA *face to face with* MAROUSSIA. *Silence.*

MAROUSSIA. Who are you? What do you want here?

He simply stares at her from behind his glasses.

KOTOV *arrives, seemingly unconcerned.*

MITIA. And finally: 3415, extension 19 arrives.

He starts singing again and feels his way to the piano stool, where he sits, raises the lid and starts to accompany himself in the stirring aria. At this moment, MAROUSSIA *recognises him. She turns away and freezes.* KOTOV *notices.* NADIA *looks at her father and shrugs. He shrugs to her. He looks again at* MAROUSSIA *who has turned back to the room and is watching* MITIA *at the piano.*

He reaches a musical climax as he removes his coat, hat, wig, glasses and finally false beard, to stand revealed before them with a flourish and a bow. General rejoicing at the return of a much-loved old friend.

OLGA. It's Mitia! Mitia!

KIRIK. It's Mitia! Of course it's Mitia! I recognised him straight away!

ELENA. Mitia! He's come back to us!

MITIA *is being hugged and having his hand shaken and his back slapped by all except* MAROUSSIA, KOTOV *and* NADIA.

LIDIA. My God, Maroussia... he's come back...

OLGA. I should've guessed, Vsevolod, because you know what he said? What Maroussia's father used to say to me when she was just a tiny girl: 'Lather will make Maroussia's skin so soft...'

VSEVOLOD (*wagging a finger at him*). Dmitri Andreevich, I must say to you... this is no way to arrive –

But MAROUSSIA *stops his mouth and stands smiling at* MITIA. *She's got over the shock and is pleased to see him. But there's trepidation too.*

MITIA. Vsevolod Konstantinovich. I completely agree with you. As always. This was no way to arrive... home.

He and MAROUSSIA *are facing one another again.*

MAROUSSIA. Well. Hello. Mitia.

MITIA. Hello. Maroussia.

He holds out a hand, palm up. She puts hers onto it. They play the childhood game of making a tower of hands. Then he kisses her hands. It's a physical shock to her. Silence.

KIRIK (*to* KOTOV). Serguei. Mitia has come back.

KOTOV. Yes.

MITIA *kisses* MAROUSSIA *on both cheeks. She's uncertain how she feels about this.*

MAROUSSIA. This is Serguei. My husband. This is the famous Mitia. The one my father was so fond of.

LIDIA. His best student.

KOTOV. Kotov.

MITIA. Delighted.

KOTOV. Same here.

They shake hands.

MITIA. Though we've already met, of course.

KOTOV. Yes.

MAROUSSIA. You have? When?

MITIA. Very briefly. A long time ago. And this is...?

MAROUSSIA. Our daughter, Nadia.

MITIA. Nadia. Call me Uncle Mitia, will you?

He kisses her hand.

NADIA. Hello, Uncle Mitia.

OLGA (*beaming*). 'Uncle Mitia'...

VSEVOLOD. Kirik...

KIRIK (*staring at* MAROUSSIA). Mm?

VSEVOLOD. Your mouth is hanging open again. Most unattractive!

MITIA spots MOKHOVA at the back.

MITIA. Mokhova... Mokhova...

She comes forward, bashfully.

MOKHOVA. Dmitri Andreevich...

MITIA. My immaculate Mokhova. Tell me. You are still immaculate, aren't you?

Much laughter. She's embarrassed but not hurt. She's charmed, like everybody except KOTOV. *He climbs onto the piano stool.*

Mokhova, Mokhova, wherefore art thou, Mokhova…?

She's like a bashful girl again. Laughter.

And why do you never dust the house properly?

MOKHOVA. What? Are you saying I don't clean the house?

Laughter, and support for her. He calls for order in the room.

MITIA. No, no, no, wait a minute, wait a minute, everybody. On New Year's Eve 1924, just before I left this house, we had hidden little gifts all around the room. I hid a sweet for Maroussia. Right here.

He points to a wall clock near him. He starts to run his hand along the top of it. He produces a sweet. He drops it onto MOKHOVA's tray. She is mortified. The others think it hilarious – even KOTOV.

MOKHOVA (*leaving*). It's a happy day for everybody except me.

VSEVOLOD *manages to squeeze her bottom as she goes.*

MAROUSSIA. Some coffee, Mokhova.

KIRIK. With a drop of something to celebrate Mitia's return.

They start to move out onto the verandah.

OLGA. I didn't recognise him at all!

MITIA *hangs back, tidying up his belongings.*
MAROUSSIA *and he are the last in the room. They stand for a second.*

He looks around the room slowly, taking it all in.

MITIA. Home.

MAROUSSIA's *elation has turned to anxiety. She walks out onto the verandah.*

Scene Six

On the verandah are LIDIA, ELENA, OLGA, VSEVOLOD, MAROUSSIA *and* KIRIK. MITIA *joins them and lights a cigarette from a silver cigarette case.* LIDIA *and* ELENA *have been wondering about something.*

LIDIA. Mitia...?

MITIA. Lidia Stepanovna...

A beat.

ELENA. What she means is... Mitia, are you married?

A beat. He smokes.

MITIA. Yes.

ELENA *nods. She thought so.* MAROUSSIA *doesn't look at him.*

LIDIA. Children?

MITIA. Yes.

ELENA. How many?

A beat. Now MAROUSSIA *looks at him.*

MITIA. Three?

OLGA. Boys?

MITIA. Boys. Oh yes: boys.

KIRIK. Bravo! Do you still play the piano?

MITIA. No.

VSEVOLOD. You just heard him play the piano, Kirik.

KIRIK. I meant, for a living. He knows what I meant. Don't you, Mitia?

MITIA. Yes. I play the piano for a living.

A beat.

VSEVOLOD. So...? Where have you – ?

MITIA. Marousse, could you give me a glass of water, please?

MAROUSSIA *pours a glass of water.*

VSEVOLOD. What I mean is... all these years, Dmitri Andreevich... Why did you never...?

OLGA. Vsevolod. Sssh. Coffee? Where's the coffee?

MITIA. What? Why did I never... what?

MAROUSSIA *absent-mindedly drinks the water herself.*

VSEVOLOD. Nothing.

Silence. Enter NADIA.

NADIA. Uncle Mitia. Tea with jam? Or coffee with milk?

MITIA. Coffee with jam.

NADIA. You cannot have coffee with jam! Coffee and jam don't go together.

OLGA. Nadia...

MITIA. Who says they don't?

NADIA. Ha!

MITIA. Ha! How old are you, Nadia?

NADIA. Nearly ten.

A beat. He looks at MAROUSSIA.

MITIA. Nearly ten. Fancy that.

MAROUSSIA *starts drumming her fingers on the glass.*

Nearly ten years old. Olga Nikolaevna.

OLGA. Yes, Mitia...?

MITIA. One day, when Maroussia was nearly ten... and I was... seventeen, the Bolshoi was performing *Lakmé* and her father Boris Konstaninovich was conducting. During the overture she said to me, 'I want to pee.' I said, 'Marousse, it's only just started.' She said, 'I want to pee.'

KOTOV arrives and stands quietly to one side, observing and listening.

People all around are shushing us up. Do you remember, Maroussia?

She is in reverie, still tapping her nails on the glass.

MAROUSSIA. No... I can't remember...

MITIA. Of course you do. So I took her out. She says, 'I can't go alone.' Now what do I do? I can't go in the ladies' without starting a riot. So. I take her in the men's room. Who is there, just getting ready to leave...?

They are enjoying the story. MITIA picks up his trumpet and starts playing some Rachmaninoff.

KIRIK. Tchaikovsky!

MITIA. Rachmaninoff! He says to me, 'Who is the father of this beautiful boy?' And I say, 'Boris Konstantinovich.' And he says, 'Then tell Boris Konstantinovich to buy him some trousers.'

Laughter, not least from KOTOV. MITIA drops into the rocking chair, near to MAROUSSIA.

NADIA. That's Pappa's chair!

KOTOV. Nadia, shame on you. He's a guest.

NADIA. You never let Kirik sit there.

MOKHOVA brings in coffee.

KOTOV. Nadia?

She looks at him. He puts his finger to his lips. NADIA sits at the table and eats a cake. The GRANNIES also eat cake with their coffee. VSEVOLOD has the newspaper again.

VSEVOLOD. Dmitri…?

MITIA. Mm…?

VSEVOLOD. In yesterday's *Pravda*… they're talking about this trial and they say 'Confession is the source of all – '

LIDIA. Vsevolod.

MITIA. Who is talking…?

VSEVOLOD. The State Prosecutor, of course.

ELENA. Vsevolod…

VSEVOLOD. I was only going to ask Dmitri Andreevich his opinion…

OLGA. Mitia? Coffee?

MITIA. No. Thank you. I asked for water.

He looks at MAROUSSIA. *They all do. Her tapping continues.*

OLGA. Maroussia? Is there something you want?

MAROUSSIA. Me? No.

OLGA. What's that then?

MAROUSSIA. This? It's a glass.

She places it on the table. Silence, except for NADIA *and her cake. Eventually:*

KOTOV. It's time for our swim!

NADIA. Hurrah! A swim!

KOTOV. Why don't we all go? Nadia! Costume! Kirik!

KIRIK. Yes, General?!

KOTOV. Swim!

KIRIK (*saluting*). Yes, General!

NADIA, KIRIK *and* KOTOV *leave.*

VSEVOLOD *unfolds the paper and reads. Silence.*

MITIA. So. I can see that everything is just as it used to be.

Silence.

ELENA. Everything changed, Mitia.

Silence.

LIDIA. The house... used to be ours. Now... we are allowed...

Silence.

MITIA. Maroussia.

She looks at him.

MAROUSSIA. Mm?

MITIA. May I have a glass of water, please?

She stares at him. She leaves abruptly.

End of Act One.

ACT TWO

Scene One

On the riverbank. The lights reveal – on a big blanket –
MAROUSSIA *in a bathing costume, lying on her front, reading
a book.*

MITIA *is sitting nearby, smoking, barefoot.*

NADIA*'s dolls are near to* MAROUSSIA.

KOTOV *is standing, looking offstage towards the river.*

MOKHOVA *is sitting on her own blanket, with crayons and
paper. She is drawing the hand that was kissed.*

LIDIA, ELENA *and* OLGA *are dozing/reading in deckchairs,
with parasols to protect them from the strong sun.*

MITIA *takes an interest in* MOKHOVA*'s drawing.*

MITIA. Mokhova, why are you drawing your hand?

> *She smiles shyly.*

MOKHOVA. A man… kissed it.

MITIA. Ah. You have a lover? No hope for me now…

MOKHOVA. No. Just the stranger who arrived just before you,
Dmitri Andreevich.

> MITIA *is a little suspicious.*

MITIA. What stranger was this, Mokhova?

MOKHOVA. He said he'd lost his way. He asked who lived in
the dacha.

MITIA. I see. Did he give his name?

MOKHOVA (*wistfully*). No.

MITIA. What did he look like?

MOKHOVA. I don't know. Handsome. He wore a cap.

Silence. All is peaceful, until:

TANNOY (*deafening*). Today at 5 pm in The Storming of the Bastille Park, there will be a performance of works by Communist composer Miniaev –

It's so loud it wakes the GRANNIES *up with a jolt. They are disoriented for a while.*

– in honour of the sixth anniversary of the construction of Comrade Stalin's balloons and airships. Admission free. Happy holiday, dear Comrades!

MITIA. Happy holiday!

MAROUSSIA. Serguei…? Can you see her?

KOTOV. Yes.

MAROUSSIA. The sun, Serguei…

KOTOV. I'll take her bonnet to her in a minute.

MAROUSSIA. The sun's too strong, Serguei…

KOTOV. Let her watch the Pioneers. She's happy. She can't wait to grow up.

MAROUSSIA. Mokhova…?

KOTOV. I'll do it, Marousse. Just be patient.

He stoops to pick up the bonnet. He's near MITIA *now.*

Mitia.

MITIA. Serguei.

Silence.

KOTOV. You're a very good singer. I'd heard it mentioned before. What was that you were singing?

MITIA (*wasn't it obvious?*). Puccini.

KOTOV. Of course. Maroussia thinks I'm a little... uneducated. A little bit coarse. Do I seem rude to you?

MITIA. Forceful...?

MAROUSSIA. He said he'd wipe his arse on the tank commanders...

Someone is blowing shrilly on a whistle somewhere, off.

(*Irritated.*) Do they have to make so much noise?

KOTOV. The Pioneers are making their pledges.

More whistle-blowing, off. He salutes.

To rise at the bugle's call. To swim at the whistle's blast.

MITIA. To march to the beat of the drum. To eat when you're told. And if you do all that... be buried to the sound of music.

KOTOV *looks at him.* MAROUSSIA *listens keenly while pretending to read. A beat.*

MAROUSSIA. Serguei, the sun...

KOTOV. Yes. I'm going. I'll take Nadia for a swim. You can have time to talk.

But he doesn't go. ELENA, OLGA *and* LIDIA *are fast asleep once more.* MOKHOVA *continues drawing her hand intently.*

MITIA. You were saying, Serguei. Why would I think you rude?

KOTOV. Well, I haven't asked you any questions. I'm not a conversationalist normally.

MITIA. No.

KOTOV. But tell us. Where have you been all this time? Eight years? Nine years?

MAROUSSIA. Eleven.

KOTOV. Eleven years. She remembers perfectly.

MITIA. Travelling. Have you been to France, Comrade?

KOTOV. No.

MITIA. Italy perhaps?

KOTOV. No. I've never left the USSR.

MITIA. Ah. Well. I sang in cabaret. When people asked me to sing. I danced. When people asked me to dance. I played piano for whoever paid to hear me.

Silence.

KOTOV. Until one day you just had to come back.

MITIA. That's it.

KOTOV. Maybe the phone rang one day. Somebody offering you a job. 'Come back, Dmitri Andreevich, we need you'…?

A beat.

MITIA. No.

KOTOV. No?

MITIA. No. One day I decided to come home.

KOTOV. Home.

Silence.

Marousse, how's your novel?

It's clear she's caught out, listening.

MAROUSSIA. Mm? Oh. Good.

He sits near her. He takes her feet onto his lap.

KOTOV. Soft feet. Like a baby's. Round and plump and soft.

MAROUSSIA. Not like yours. Hard and rough.

KOTOV. Not like mine: hard and rough.

MITIA. Comrade Kotov has walked a lot in his life.

KOTOV. Sometimes. Sometimes I ran. It depended how
quickly they were retreating. But that's all over now. That's
all over. Now we're building cars and roads. And trains.
And trolley-buses, and underground trains. And aeroplanes
and airships. So that Maroussia here and Nadia will always
have soft feet. All their lives, soft feet. That's why we're
doing it.

He's stroking her feet, while maintaining eye contact with
MITIA. MAROUSSIA *becomes uncomfortable and sits up.*

MAROUSSIA. You were tickling me.

A beat.

KOTOV. Was I? I'm sorry. Your feet are so soft. You've no
idea, Maroussia, how good it feels to touch you.

Eye contact with her. She looks away. He gets up and takes
the bonnet again.

Well. The sun. A swim. Why don't you join us when you feel
like it? When you've had a chance to talk about old times?
Oh. What time will you be leaving?

MITIA *spreads his hands wide. He doesn't know.* KOTOV
leaves.

Scene Two

MITIA *stands and looks around.*

ELENA, LIDIA *and* OLGA *are all asleep.*

MOKHOVA *is still drawing her hand.*

TANNOY (*deafening*). Please return the poodle called
Philomon to the janitor of dacha number seventeen –
Professor Kaluta's home. Happy holiday, dear Comrades.

This time the ladies sleep on.

MITIA. Happy holiday. Olga Nikolaievna…?

She doesn't stir. He calls louder, in her ear.

Olga Nikolaievna…?!

OLGA (*waking with a start*). Mm? There was no need to shout, I wasn't asleep.

MITIA. Olga Nikolaievna, do you remember when I first came to live with you and learn music – when Maroussia was this big – ?

He has one of NADIA*'s dolls sitting on his hand.*

And you led me to her crib to meet her for the first time? Tiny creature. I held my finger out towards her hand and she grabbed it.

OLGA. Yes.

MITIA. And she whispered to me, 'Come closer, Mitia, come closer. Sing to me.' So I sang to her for the first time. And she smiled and said, 'More, Mitia, more. Again. Again.'

OLGA*'s nostalgic smile goes.* MAROUSSIA *seems disturbed.*

OLGA. No, I can't remember… What are you talking about? How could she talk when she was in her crib?

MITIA. Yes, that is odd, isn't it? Maybe I'm mixing it up with some other occasion. Maroussia, do you remember? Maybe I dreamed it.

ELENA *and* LIDIA *are waking up.*

OLGA. Mother, a swim? Elena?

LIDIA. Yes, Elena, let's swim.

All three disrobe demurely, revealing swimsuits. They sing with one another as they do so.

OLGA/LIDIA/ELENA (*singing*).
> But it's a real shame,
> You ran off to travel the world,
> And I followed, true to my word,
> Oh, oh, oh… Tchouki-tchouki-tchouki –

They are gone, towards the river. MITIA *sits with* MAROUSSIA.

MITIA. Well. Maroussia. It is not only your husband who is rude. You too.

MAROUSSIA. Why?

MITIA. You don't ask me any questions either.

Silence.

Then I'll ask.

He takes her hand and looks at her arms. His finger traces the scars.

What are these scars?

Silence. She retrieves her hand.

MAROUSSIA. You left without a word and you didn't come back. Anyway, they stopped me. I did it wrong. I didn't know you had to do it in warm water.

KOTOV *enters, at a distance.*

KOTOV. Marousse. We're taking the boat along the river.

MAROUSSIA. Be careful, I don't like –

KOTOV. Maroussia. Just let us go. Leave us alone together. Lie there in the sun.

A beat. He goes.

MITIA. Wide, muscular shoulders. Really, I understand. A dazzling smile. His portrait hanging everywhere you look. Yes, really, I understand.

Some accordion music, off. He takes off his shirt. There's a livid scar on his chest and shoulder.

MAROUSSIA. You didn't have that. Before.

MITIA. What...?

She reaches out to touch it. He flinches at first and then he lets her.

MAROUSSIA. That...

MITIA. Oh, that. It's nothing. The lid grazed me, that's all.

MAROUSSIA. What lid?

MITIA. The coffin lid. Somebody didn't like my singing.

MAROUSSIA. Mitia, why have you come back? What's the point of it now?

MITIA. Why?

A pause.

MAROUSSIA. I'm going for a swim.

She stands. He holds onto her hand. He won't let go.

Let me go, Mitia.

MITIA. Why?

MAROUSSIA. What would your wife say?

MITIA. I have no wife, Maroussia.

He pulls her back down.

MAROUSSIA. No wife? But I heard you telling –

MITIA. You heard me telling stories. You heard me being what the old ladies want me to be.

MAROUSSIA. I don't understand, Mitia. Why have you come back now?

MITIA. Do you remember this place? Maroussia? This exact place...?

A pause.

MAROUSSIA. Yes.

MITIA. One month after Boris Konstantinovich died, you
    caught your mother with Kirik. A terrible business. Kirik – of
    all people. You were devastated. You ran out of the house –
    and I found you here later that night. Right there. Staring at
    the water. It was cold. It was raining. I told you to go back,
    but you didn't want to. So I stayed with you. Do you
    remember?

A beat.

MAROUSSIA. Yes. I remember.

MITIA. Then you remember how we spent the night together in
    the boatman's barn? Our first night. You were wild. Wild
    with grief. You needed more and more and more. And
    afterwards I talked to you for hours. About your father. You
    didn't know how you would ever live without him. And how
    could death have taken him so unfairly? And I read you
    Aeschylus. Do you remember?

She nods.

'Even in our sleep the pain that cannot forget falls drop by
drop upon the heart until – in our despair and against our will
– wisdom comes through the awful grace of God.'

MAROUSSIA. You went away.

MITIA. I didn't abandon you, Maroussia. I did not abandon
    you. But why have you deleted me?

MAROUSSIA. Tell me why you've come back…?

MITIA. I don't know. Perhaps… because I believed that if life
    no longer existed for me, then it no longer existed for
    anybody. Perhaps because I believed that it wasn't just me
    that vanished. Everybody vanished. But… here you all are.
    And nothing has changed for you at all. Except that I'm not
    here. You've obliterated me, Maroussia… taken me out of
    the picture. Forgotten me.

Silence. She faces him. Her hand touches his face.

MAROUSSIA (*quietly*). Never. Not for one hour of one day.

Are they going to kiss? Enter the DRIVER *again. He sees* MITIA. *He's still lost, still clutching his piece of paper.*

DRIVER. Sir? Sir? Excuse me…?

MAROUSSIA *breaks away. The* DRIVER *sees* MOKHOVA *staring at him.*

MAROUSSIA. I'm going for a swim.

DRIVER. Ah…

MITIA (*pointing to* MOKHOVA). Yonder lies your love. Maroussia…?

He follows her off. The DRIVER *approaches* MOKHOVA. *Silence.*

DRIVER. Hello again.

MOKHOVA. Hello.

DRIVER. I don't suppose this is…

MOKHOVA. Zagorienka…? No.

DRIVER. Or Zagorienko?

MOKHOVA. No. It's where you were this morning. The dacha's just up the hill.

DRIVER. I thought it seemed familiar.

He sits and looks at her drawings. She's embarrassed by this and by his proximity. He takes out his lunch, wrapped in a handkerchief. He eats gherkins and hard bread. He offers her some. She hesitates and accepts. They eat.

All alone?

MOKHOVA. No.

He looks around the deserted riverbank and nods.

DRIVER. Did you read about the fireballs?

MOKHOVA. Fireballs?

He takes out a folded newspaper and reads to her.

DRIVER. 'Undesirable guests. Over the last two weeks there
have been, in the Moscow area, several sightings of fireballs.
These undesirable guests disappear as fast as they arrive –
but only after damaging the property and the physical bodies
of the workers.' Think. The physical bodies. That means
these fireballs have been crashing into people, burning them
to ashes. 'These – '

*He can't read the next word. He offers the paper to her,
pointing.*

MOKHOVA. 'Phenomena.'

DRIVER. 'Phenomena'?

MOKHOVA. Mm.

DRIVER. 'These – phenomena – are caused by a well-
organised diversionary programme on behalf of imperialist
terrorists.' Think.

*He stares at her. She stares at him, wondering what next.
Silence. Suddenly, tears well in his eyes.*

What's your name?

MOKHOVA. Mokhova.

DRIVER. Mokhova. I'm lost, Mokhova. I don't know where to
go any more. Do you think anybody can help me?

A siren shatters the air.

TANNOY. Gas warning! We are under attack!

The riverbank fills with the PIONEERS *and their adult*
OFFICERS, *wearing gas masks and carrying stretchers.*

Civil Defence and Pioneers will protect you from the
Imperialist foe! Happy holiday!

OLGA, ELENA *and* LIDIA *come back in a hurry as martial
music plays through the Tannoy system. They are having gas
masks foisted on them and* PIONEERS *are trying to get them
to lie on the stretchers so they can practise. The* GRANNIES
push them away.

LIDIA. Get off me!

OLGA. Leave us alone!

They're trying to dry themselves.

ELENA. Mokhova! Don't let them put you on a stretcher! Did you see Mitia? He jumped into the river beside Maroussia! Fully clothed! Who is your man friend?

The DRIVER *is completely terrified. He runs away.*

MOKHOVA. He's not my man friend! I'm a maiden.

OLGA. The whole district knows that, Mokhova. Get off me! What gas?! How can there be gas out here?

MOKHOVA *comes face to face with two* PIONEERS *wearing gas masks. They are hideous and frightening, like zombies with elephant trunks. She screams and runs away.*

MAROUSSIA *runs on, wet through.*

MAROUSSIA. Hey! I'm injured!

OFFICER. You're injured?

MAROUSSIA. Yep.

OFFICER. Bad?

MAROUSSIA. Yep.

OFFICER. Get on this stretcher.

MAROUSSIA. Yep.

She grabs her novel and lies on the stretcher. They put a gas mask on her. She throws her novel down as they carry her away.

MITIA *arrives, fully clothed and dripping wet.*

OLGA, ELENA *and* LIDIA *are leaving with their things.*

MITIA. Take me! I'm a dead body.

OFFICER. Are you hurt?

MITIA. Quite badly.

*He sits on a stretcher, putting on a gas mask, and is carried
away. The music has ended. The place is empty and quiet. A
beat. Then:*

TANNOY. It is the duty of every Soviet citizen to help Civilian
Defence fight the hydra of world Imperialism. Happy
holiday, dear Comrades.

Scene Three

Enter KOTOV *and* NADIA, *hand in hand, wondering where
everybody went in such a hurry. There are abandoned
belongings everywhere.*

NADIA. Where have Mamma and Uncle Mitia gone?

KOTOV. I've no idea. How would I know?

NADIA. Look, Pappa, they went without their shoes. Let's run
after them.

KOTOV. No. Nadia. Sit. Sit a while. Let them… talk.

He sits in a chair. She sits on his lap.

NADIA. I like Uncle Mitia.

KOTOV. Mm. Ssh. You're hot. You're not feeling ill, are you?

NADIA. No.

KOTOV. Are you sad?

NADIA. No. I'm never sad about anything when I'm with you.
Why have they left us?

KOTOV. They want to talk together. They're old friends. He
has a story to tell her.

NADIA. A story?

KOTOV. Uh-huh.

NADIA. What is the story?

KOTOV. I don't know it. It's his story, not mine.

She puts her cheek on his.

NADIA. Will today go on for ever?

KOTOV. Would you like it to?

She nods.

NADIA. You've no idea how good it feels to be with you.

A pause.

KOTOV. Each day must end, Nadia. But more days come after. Remember that. And those days make a path. Follow your path. Follow it well. Work hard. Respect your parents and teachers. And above all, Nadia, cherish your Soviet motherland.

NADIA. I adore you.

KOTOV. With you, everything is calm. And easy.

She's hugging her face into his neck.

Perhaps this day will just drift for ever. Like the boat on the river. Would you like that?

NADIA. Yes. As long as we can have Mamma in our boat.

KOTOV. Of course. We wouldn't leave her behind.

Silence.

Shall we go and find her, Nadia?

Piano music takes us over into:

Scene Four

The music room. MITIA – *in borrowed dressing gown and still wearing his gas mask – is at the piano along with* MAROUSSIA – *in a simple white dress now and also wearing her gas mask. They are playing together. Puccini again. Standing or sitting around are* VSEVOLOD, OLGA, LIDIA *and* ELENA – *chattering and laughing under the music.*

NADIA *arrives from outside, taking off her sun bonnet. She stands near the piano, smiling.*

OLGA. I remember… Boris had decided to give work to a poor student – Mitia. His job was to make Maroussia work harder on her music – she was such a lazy girl.

MAROUSSIA *would look outraged if she weren't wearing the mask.*

And as long as I was here in this room keeping an eye on them, they were serious. Legato… syncopated pedal… appoggiatura… But…

MAROUSSIA *takes off her mask, laughing, knowing what's coming. They are still playing, but the tune is morphing, led by her.*

MAROUSSIA. But…

OLGA. Yes, *but*, one day – I'd only just stepped out of the room but they thought they were safe…

'Ooooohs' and 'Aaaaahs' of mock concern as they all remember with pleasure the story that's coming.

KOTOV *arrives in a linen suit. He stands apart, watching and listening.*

And when I come back in, what do I hear…?

MAROUSSIA *is already picking out the first notes of the can-can.*

Mitia! You must remember!

*They both start playing the can-can, quite slowly at first –
but then picking up speed.*

MAROUSSIA. The can-can! Mother came back into the room.
I was Nadia's age…

*She turns round on the piano stool, facing them, and starts
lifting her dress to the knee and kicking her feet.*

OLGA. I thought I was going to faint!

MAROUSSIA. And I was doing this!

OLGA (*copying her*). And with great style for a ten-year-old!

MAROUSSIA *shrieks with pleasure at the memory and
stands to dance.* MITIA *picks up the tempo and the volume
as the others join in the dance.*

KOTOV *looks on.*

Shrieks of delight from MAROUSSIA *and* NADIA *as they
hold hands and dance a full-blown can-can.*

KIRIK *arrives, running.*

KIRIK. They're dancing! Why didn't you call me?!

KOTOV (*above the music*). Because I don't speak French!

KIRIK *joins in, enthusiastically.* MOKHOVA *arrives.*

MOKHOVA (*shouting*). Serguei Petrovich! Shall I serve lunch?
Serguei Petrovich! Shall I serve lunch?!

*He ignores her. He watches the dancing and the menacing
figure of* MITIA, *orchestrating the wildness. He seems to be
staring straight at* KOTOV. *His playing becomes slightly
discordant and mad; quicker and quicker, louder and
louder.*

Lunch! Lunch is ready!

VSEVOLOD. Lunch!

KIRIK. Lunch!

MAROUSSIA. No, no! More! More!

KIRIK *leads the dance out towards the dining room.*
MAROUSSIA *dances on alone, madly, spinning.*

KOTOV *stays.*

MITIA *goes on playing. Very loud, very mad, very*
menacing. He suddenly stops.

Don't stop, Mitia! More, more, again, again!

She sees KOTOV. *She stops dancing. She regains her*
senses. She leaves.

MITIA *and* KOTOV *look at one another as* MITIA
continues the music of madness.

Blackout.

End of Act Two.

ACT THREE

Scene One

On the verandah.

They have eaten lunch. KOTOV*'s rocking chair is empty because he's leaning against the wall. Everyone else is around the table, finishing off coffee, smoking, and listening to* ELENA, *who is singing 'One Fine Day' from* Madame Butterfly *(...one day soon her true love will sail his ship into the harbour and they will be reunited).* NADIA *is on* MAROUSSIA's *lap, holding her dolls. The aria ends. They applaud gently but enthusiastically. The mood is elegaic and wistful.*

ELENA. Oh... my voice is gone.

LIDIA. Nonsense – it was just like when you sang in the theatre.

VSEVOLOD. Exquisite. Exquisite, Elena Mikhailovna. The rest is silence.

NADIA. Pappa said Uncle Mitia has a story for me.

MITIA. A story...?

KOTOV. Not for you, Nadia. For Marousse.

MITIA. I don't remember mentioning a story.

KOTOV. No? And yet I'm certain you have a story to tell.

NADIA. Yes, Uncle Mitia, tell us your story.

KOTOV. Perhaps you could tell it in French or Italian if that's easier for you...?

Silence.

LIDIA. Perhaps Dmitri Andreevich cannot think of a story...

KOTOV. Of course he can. Why doesn't he tell us where he's been and what he's been doing? Choose any language you want, Mitia.

A pause.

MITIA. A story. A fairy story.

ALL. Ah.

NADIA. Hurrah! A fairy story. Like the Pioneers' song: 'We come to make the fairy tales come true!'...

MITIA *sits opposite* MAROUSSIA.

MITIA. Very well. Nadia. Bring me your dolls.

She takes her dolls and goes to sit on MITIA's *lap.*

KOTOV. Nadia.

KOTOV *beckons her on to his lap instead.* MITIA *looks at* MAROUSSIA *and smiles. She smiles back.*

MITIA. So. How should the fairy story begin, Maroussia?

NADIA. 'Once upon a time...'

KOTOV. Nadia. It's not your story.

MITIA. Of course. Once upon a time. When wishing still helped. In the land of Iassur.

MAROUSSIA. Iassur. Where's that?

MITIA. Not far away. In the land of Iassur. There was a little boy... called Iatim.

MAROUSSIA. Iatim. What a strange name.

He takes one of the dolls and stands it on the table.

MITIA. Iatim. He sang beautifully. Played piano, guitar. Loved poetry, Shakespeare... His parents were not rich, but they had a friend who was a kind magician. His name was Sirob.

He stands up another doll.

MAROUSSIA. Did Sirob have a magic wand?

MITIA. Yes… in fact, he did. He waved it and it made beautiful music. And Sirob liked little Iatim very much and was kind to him. He took him into his house to teach him all he knew about magic. And music. Iatim loved Sirob like a son loves his father. And vice versa. Sirob had a daughter.

MAROUSSIA *hands him a girl doll.*

Thank you. He called her –

MAROUSSIA (*laughing*). Don't tell me. Iassouram?

MITIA. What a good idea. Iassouram.

NADIA. That's a silly name.

She's losing interest. She rests her head on KOTOV's *shoulder, puts her thumb in her mouth and gradually falls asleep.*

MITIA. Iatim thought so too. Sirob had a big house. Very bright, very merry… and of course – very happy.

LIDIA. Like ours.

MITIA. Like ours. Like yours. But one day all this came to an end: no more tea drunk from china cups, no more charades, no more croquet on the lawn. Which of course is a bourgeois game. Like tennis.

MAROUSSIA *tuts her mock disapproval.*

KIRIK. We play football these days. Serguei Petrovich says that's a team game. For everybody to play.

LIDIA. Can you imagine, Mitia? At our age, he makes us to play football…

MITIA. Uh-huh? Well, Serguei Petrovich should know all about team games. He played for the winning team.

He smiles at KOTOV. *The others chuckle and rib him.* KOTOV *appears to take it in good part, but his eyes are not smiling.*

But – in the house of Sirob the Magician... no more laughter, no more sunny days... and all the rest. It all ended.

MAROUSSIA. Why?

MITIA. Because war came to the land.

MAROUSSIA. How could that be helped?

MITIA. That doesn't matter. The thing is, that Iatim left home and went to war. And all that time, in the trenches, in the hospital, all that time in all the land he crossed while the war was being won and lost, every day, every single day, he thought about the big house, the garden, the verandah, the river... everything. That's all he could think about.

NADIA *is asleep. The others are listening intently as the tone of the story has changed.* MITIA *stands abruptly.*

Want some vodka, Kirik?

KIRIK. Erm...

ELENA. He doesn't drink.

KIRIK. Well... special occasions.

MITIA. Special occasions. Just so. Why don't you open us a bottle?

KIRIK *does so. And pours two glasses.*

And so. For five years, Iatim was a soldier. He roamed far and wide in his benighted country. Far and wide. Good health.

He downs his drink in one. KIRIK *does likewise and pours them a second. He offers one to* KOTOV, *who shakes his head.*

And all the while he thought of that house where he had been so happy. Good health.

He drinks. KIRIK *drinks then goes to pour another for* MITIA *who covers his glass with his hand.* KIRIK *hesitates, then pours himself another.* ELENA *is glaring at him. He*

shrugs at her as if saying, 'What else was I supposed to do?'
MITIA *lights a cigarette.*

Then one day – after five years – he came back. Five years.
His parents had died during the war. The war that couldn't be
helped. So he had nowhere to go – except to the kind
magician's house. He went. It was winter, and apart from the
snow, he recognised nothing of this world he had been so
happy in as a boy. It had changed completely. Only the big
house was there like before. All of a tremble, he tapped on
the door.

He drums his fingers on his glass, like MAROUSSIA *did
earlier.*

A young girl answered. Iatim had never seen anybody so
beautiful.

He stands the dolls so they face each other.

Ever. Even though he had travelled a lot. 'Who are you?'
asked Iatim. 'Iassouram,' answered the beautiful girl. 'Good
Lord, not the same Iassouram who slept on her father's knee
when he was teaching me music?' 'Yes, I am she. Come in.
We've been waiting for you for a long, long time, even
though Pappa is very ill now.'

He knocks one doll down.

Iatim was astounded. He couldn't say a word. Not a word.

MAROUSSIA *pours some vodka for herself with a shaking
hand. She knocks it back.*

They fell in love. Of course.

KIRIK. Of course.

ELENA (*shutting him up*). Kirik.

Silence.

MAROUSSIA. But how did the story end? All good stories
should have a happy ending, shouldn't they?

MITIA. Well. No. Actually. Sometimes they can't.

MAROUSSIA. Why not?

MITIA. Because... one fine day a very important man sent for
Iatim.

MAROUSSIA. Oh, who is this? The bogeyman?

MITIA. No, he wasn't quite that important.

MAROUSSIA. An ogre.

MITIA. Not that frightening either. I've forgotten his name
now.

KIRIK. Doesn't matter.

MITIA. Doesn't matter. But he summoned Iatim to the big
palace in Wocsom and said to him, 'Comrade Iatim. There is
something you must do for me. Far away. Don't ask where.
Don't ask what.'

KIRIK. Doesn't matter.

MITIA. Doesn't matter. But Iatim replied, 'Sir, I've already
fought so hard. I've already travelled so far and longed for
home. Can't I just be quiet here in this land that's become so
different? Can't I live in peace with those I love?' And this
very important man said, 'Those ideas, my dear Iatim, are
bourgeois.'

KIRIK. Like croquet.

MITIA. Like croquet. Or Puccini. Terrible. Unforgiveable.
Reactionary. 'We can't let you go back to that house and
turn it once more into a middle-class nest for people like
you who think only about the past... and how comfortable it
was. It's time you were a team player, working for the good
of all.' So... Iatim thought a lot and wondered what the
important man would do to him if he refused the tasks he
was given.

MAROUSSIA *is getting very disturbed.* KOTOV *doesn't
take his eyes off her.*

And packed his bags and left. Without a word to anyone.

MAROUSSIA. Not one word to Iassouram?

MITIA. No.

MAROUSSIA. Why not?

A pause.

MITIA. Because he didn't know what to say to her. His life had been full of blood and death. He didn't want to bring all that to the happy house. And also, Maroussia, because he was only twenty-five. And he really... really wanted to go on living.

MAROUSSIA. What about Iassouram? In this story. What happened to her?

MITIA. Iassouram? She cried. And then she cried again. And then she cried again. More and more and again and again. And then she got married.

MAROUSSIA. Maybe she wanted to live too.

Silence.

OLGA. What a sad story.

MITIA *starts whistling softly, 'The Weary Sun'. KIRIK hums it with him. Then he sings the lyrics.*

KIRIK (*singing*).
　　I heard you say, my dove,
　　That there would be no love.

MAROUSSIA *tries to pour another vodka but her hands shake too much.*

(*Singing.*)
　　Burnt by the sun,
　　As the crimson sea did run,
　　I heard you say, my dove,
　　That there would be –

MAROUSSIA. Kirik!

Silence. NADIA wakes up.

The sun. Take Nadia indoors.

NADIA. But, I'm –

MAROUSSIA. Now. Go and finish your nap.

LIDIA. Come, Nadia, we'll talk to the budgerigars on the way.

LIDIA, OLGA *and* ELENA *sweep up* NADIA *and go indoors.* VSEVOLOD *and* KIRIK *are going too.* KIRIK *picks up the bottle.*

KIRIK. Mitia? Another vodka?

Silence.

MITIA. Yes. Why not?

VSEVOLOD, KIRIK *and* MITIA *leave. Silence.* MAROUSSIA *wipes tears from her eyes.*

Scene Two

KOTOV *stares at her, waiting. She won't look at him.*

KOTOV. He had a choice.

She starts shaking her head. She's in shock. She doesn't know what to do, where to go.

We all have a choice, Maroussia.

She gets up and starts to leave through the garden. She turns back on him.

MAROUSSIA. You stole me! You cheated me!

KOTOV. No. No.

He grabs her. He holds her close. She struggles.

No.

MAROUSSIA. You sent him away. It was you.

KOTOV. Yes.

She tears herself away and runs towards the house.

Maroussia, wait!

He pursues her. She grabs a knife from the table and holds it against her wrist. He stops in his tracks.

Maroussia. There's Nadia. There's Nadia...

He moves towards her.

MAROUSSIA. Stay there!

A pause.

KOTOV. Maroussia. Come here. Come here, my love.

He walks slowly towards her. He takes off his jacket and his shirt.

MAROUSSIA. No.

KOTOV. Come here.

MAROUSSIA. No.

He reaches out his hand and touches her cheek. His other hand takes the knife from her and drops it.

KOTOV. There. Come here.

MAROUSSIA. No.

He unbuttons her dress and uncovers her to the waist. He draws her close to him in an embrace. He sinks onto a chair and pulls her down gently so that she is straddling him. He pulls up her dress, exposing her legs.

Wait. Wait. What are you doing?

KOTOV. Why, Marousse...?

MAROUSSIA. What are you doing?

KOTOV. Not here? Why not? Who would be shocked? Would any of them even be surprised? They think of me as a barbarian.

MAROUSSIA. You are.

KOTOV. I'm not like them. Isn't that why you wanted me? What did you want, Maroussia? Come on. Let's go to the steam hut.

MAROUSSIA. Why should I go anywhere with you?

KOTOV. Don't you know why? My love. My love.

A pause.

MAROUSSIA. Did you know who he was when you sent him away?

KOTOV. He left of his own free will, Maroussia. He had a choice. Every one of them had a choice.

MAROUSSIA. What choice? Do the Party's bidding or face prison? Or a firing squad?

KOTOV. We all have an alternative, Maroussia. I have. You have. We can talk. We can stay silent. We can leave. We can stay. We can fight. We can run away. There is always a choice if you're prepared to pay the price for choosing.

MAROUSSIA. Why Mitia? Why him?

KOTOV. Why not him? Remember, we sent hundreds of them abroad. Thousands. To embassies, to consulates, as correspondents, as businessmen... He already knew things... he already spoke their languages. He was useful.

MAROUSSIA. As what? What did you ask him to do?

KOTOV. Ask him that. Why don't you?

A pause.

MAROUSSIA. Tell me. What if it had been you? If they'd given you that choice. Would you have gone? Would you have left me?

KOTOV. Of course. I'm a soldier. But, Maroussia, I would have left you because I love my Motherland. He left you because he was frightened to die. Do you understand the difference?

My love? There's duty. And there's fear. You have to understand the difference. Do you understand?

A pause.

MAROUSSIA. Yes. I understand. The Party will always come first.

She pulls herself free of him and buttons her dress. He stands.

KOTOV. Ask him. Ask him why he left. Ask him what he did out of fear. Tell him, this time you don't want to hear a fairy story.

A pause.

Will you come with me to the steam hut, Marousse?

She thinks. She looks him in the eye.

MAROUSSIA. No.

He nods. He leaves.

Scene Three

MITIA *wanders through the music room. He stops at the piano to play some Puccini. On the verandah,* MAROUSSIA *listens. He stops. He comes out and joins her.*

MITIA. The house is asleep.

MAROUSSIA. Why didn't you come and explain? Why didn't you come and say goodbye? If you'd asked me to, I'd've followed you anywhere.

MITIA. Because, Maroussia, it was forbidden. I was given one hour to decide. Do this work for the Party or...

MAROUSSIA. Did he know about us?

MITIA. Before? I don't think so. I don't think Serguei wanted
to steal you. It was nothing personal. He was serving the
Party. Did I tell him about us? Yes. I begged to be allowed to
stay with you and be happy. I told him your name and where
you lived. Maybe it made him curious to meet this beguiling
creature... I don't know. You tell me.

MAROUSSIA. The Party offered him our dacha. He came to
look. Then he came the next week with flowers. Every week
for six months.

MITIA. Six months...

MAROUSSIA. Tell me about Paris.

MITIA. There's nothing to say. It was beautiful. But I thought
every day about what I had lost.

MAROUSSIA (*interrupting*). Tell me what you did in Paris.

MITIA. I did what they asked. I found them information...
Information is the air the Party breathes... Who talks to
who... who goes to bed with who... who has money... who
has influence...

MAROUSSIA. You could have written me a letter.

MITIA. I wrote you a hundred letters. Though I knew they'd
never reach you.

This idea moves her.

In the end I was told to stop writing. Or I would never be
allowed home.

A beat. Her hand finds his, briefly.

MAROUSSIA. But they've let you come home?

MITIA. Yes. One fine day they said, 'You can come home.'

MAROUSSIA. And what do you do now?

MITIA. Play the piano. In a restaurant in Moscow.

MAROUSSIA. I'll come and see you.

MITIA. Yes. Yes, I'd like that.

MAROUSSIA. Before you went to the front. When I was still little... you promised to dance for me.

MITIA. I did?

MAROUSSIA. Yes. Don't you remember your promise, Mitia?

He thinks. He smiles.

MITIA. Yes.

MAROUSSIA. So...?

She stands facing him.

He does a few steps of a tap routine which develop into a short sequence. She loves it.

Can you teach me that?

MITIA. I can try.

He starts to show her the steps. She follows him, picking it up well. They're both enjoying it, and the contact it brings. She's getting on well with it until he suddenly breaks off as KOTOV arrives.

MAROUSSIA. Serguei, look what Mitia is teaching me.

KOTOV. Yes.

MAROUSSIA. Tap dancing.

KOTOV. I saw.

MAROUSSIA. He's a brilliant dancer.

KOTOV. I'm sure.

MAROUSSIA. Show him, Mitia.

MITIA. Oh... Serguei Petrovich doesn't want to –

KOTOV. Yes.

MITIA. But it's... decadent... an unproductive activity...

KOTOV *shrugs*. MITIA *does his routine*. MAROUSSIA *applauds*.

MAROUSSIA. Don't you think he's brilliant?

KOTOV. Outstanding.

MAROUSSIA. I don't suppose they ever taught you to tap dance in that 'shed of a schoolroom'.

KOTOV. No.

MAROUSSIA. Teach me some more, Mitia.

KOTOV. Marousse.

MAROUSSIA. Teach me all you know. More. More.

KOTOV. Marousse.

MAROUSSIA. Again. Again.

KOTOV. Marousse!

She turns and watches. KOTOV *takes off his jacket, clears his throat, steadies himself and launches into a loudly percussive tap dance which bears some resemblance to a train picking up speed and leaving a station. He builds to an impressive climax.* MITIA *applauds loudly.*

MITIA. Bravo!

She claps too.

MAROUSSIA. Where did you learn that?

KOTOV. In the Army. Did you ask?

MAROUSSIA. Yes.

KOTOV. Was it a good story?

MAROUSSIA. Very.

KOTOV. And what was Mitia doing all that time?

MAROUSSIA. He told you when we were at the river.

KOTOV. I didn't know you were listening.

MAROUSSIA. Why shouldn't I listen?

KOTOV. Playing the piano then?

MAROUSSIA. Yes. And writing letters.

KOTOV. Writing letters as well? Did he say who to?

MAROUSSIA. Me.

She looks into his eyes.

KOTOV. You?

He turns his gaze on MITIA, *who smiles at him.*

I see. Thirsty work, this dancing. Marousse, get us a vodka,
eh? And I'll tell you who Mitia wrote letters to.

She looks at him and at MITIA.

Vodka.

She gets a bottle and three glasses.

MITIA. He snaps his fingers and you run.

KOTOV. And who he played piano for.

MAROUSSIA. What do you mean, 'who for'?

MITIA. Just like that, Maroussia.

He snaps his fingers.

KOTOV. He plays piano for the NKVD.

She looks at MITIA.

MAROUSSIA. Political police?

MITIA. You think he's a god, don't you? You believe every
word he tells you. Where is that free spirit who questioned
everybody and everything? Who played piano and sang and
danced. Where did she go to, Maroussia? The little girl who
wanted to dance. Did she learn to go to the celebrations and

play football? He might at least have built you a new prison
cell – did he have to put bars on the windows of this
beautiful place?

A pause.

KOTOV. Tell her, Mitia.

MAROUSSIA. Tell me what now?

KOTOV. Ask him what he gave us in return for his life. In
return for his ticket home.

MAROUSSIA. Why did he have to make a choice?

KOTOV. Because we all have to make it. Okay, I'll tell her.

MITIA. He'll tell you lies.

KOTOV. No, no, Andersen, I don't tell lies.

MAROUSSIA. Andersen...?

KOTOV. Yes, that fellow who tells shitty little fairy stories all
the time. All I want to know from you, Hans Christian, is
why – in your shitty little fairy story – didn't you tell
everybody that since 1924 – for the last twelve years, pretty
boy – you've worked in counter-espionage? 'Playing the
piano' for us all around Paris... where you led us to no fewer
than eight White Army generals... who – thanks to you –
were brought back to Moscow by force – drugged and
locked in trucks – and then shot. Without trials. Enemies of
the people. Why didn't you mention that?

MITIA. Because it's not true, perhaps?

KOTOV. Not true? What's not true? That they were shot or that
they were enemies of the people?

MITIA. Any of it.

KOTOV. Oh. They were shot all right, pretty boy. Don't kid
yourself about that. And they were enemies of the people all
right. You see, Maroussia: I'm allowed to say that because I
fought *against* those generals for four years.

He looks at MITIA *and waits. Nothing.*

MAROUSSIA. What's he saying, Mitia?

MITIA *shakes his head, it's all nonsense.*

MITIA. Yes, what are you saying, Comrade?

KOTOV. I'm saying, pretty boy, that you had fought *on their side*! For the White Army, with their British and French friends, to destroy the Revolution. And then – when you had to save your own neck – you turned them in to us. Betrayed eight generals. Eight fighting men. Kornev, Weiner, Machkov... all of them.

Silence. MITIA *looks at* MAROUSSIA.

MITIA. He knows better than anyone I was forced to do what I did.

KOTOV. By who, Mitia? Who forced you? Who forced you, you poor innocent? I didn't force you to do anything. I bought you. Like a whore.

MAROUSSIA. Serguei...

KOTOV. Open your eyes, Maroussia.

MITIA. You really shouldn't talk to me like that, Comrade. I never asked for money. I wanted one thing. One thing. To come back to this house, to what I'd left behind. Your friends promised it to me and I believed them. 'Go to Paris. Find these men. Do this for us and we'll let you go back.' You lied to me. You took everything I had. Everything! My life, my profession, my love, Maroussia, my country, my faith! My hope! You took it all from me. And then you moved in.

KOTOV. Ah. So that's why you've come back. To wallow in it, to revel in your pain. To savour it drop by drop, sip by sip. And then – when the glass is empty –

He stops himself.

MITIA. Comrade. You above all men know exactly why I came here.

A silence.

MAROUSSIA. What does he mean?

A silence.

KOTOV. Of course I know, Comrade. Of course I know.

MITIA. It really is nothing personal, General.

KOTOV. Of course not.

MAROUSSIA. What does he mean?

> KOTOV *simply points at* MITIA *as a warning: 'Be quiet.'*

> MITIA *shakes his head at her. Nothing. He downs his shot of vodka.*

> Mitia?

MITIA. Maroussia?

MAROUSSIA. It was the life, wasn't it, Mitia? The life, wasn't it, that you thought of every single day. Not me. But it's gone anyway, Mitia. The old people live out the memories of it... because Kotov lets them. He could make their world stop. Like that.

She snaps her fingers.

And do you know why he doesn't?

He shakes his head. But he does know.

Because he's sorry for them, perhaps? He despises them.

KOTOV. No, no...

MAROUSSIA. Yes, you do, Serguei. How could you not? Because he has a soft spot for them? Kotov has no soft spots. He is the hardest man on the planet. Ruthless in his hatred of what went before. So why does he let them come here every summer and pretend the world never changed? Because Kotov loves me with every bone in his body. That's why.

Silence. KOTOV *raises a glass to her and then to* MITIA. *He downs it.*

MITIA. You're right, Maroussia. The world really can be made to stop... just like this.

He is about to snap his fingers. He waits, looking into her eyes, making a decision. He snaps his fingers. And NADIA *appears.*

NADIA. Pappa –

MITIA. Magic.

NADIA. Is it nearly time to go to the zoo?

KOTOV. Nearly.

NADIA. Uncle Mitia, will you come to the zoo with us? I've only been in the winter when we're in Moscow and the animals are always asleep so Pappa promised to take me today when they're all awake. The grannies fainted last time we went – like this...

She drops to the floor and gets up again.

It was from the smell. Of the animals. Not the people. Will you come?

MITIA. I'm afraid I can't, Nadia. I'll be leaving soon. There's a car coming at four.

He opens his arms for her to embrace him. KOTOV *stands between them.*

KOTOV. Go with your mother, Nadia.

NADIA. But, Pappa –

KOTOV. Go.

MAROUSSIA *and* NADIA *leave.*

You're a guest here. And we can carry on playing this game until you're ready to leave. But don't touch my daughter.

MITIA. Is that an order, General?

KOTOV. She goes to the zoo with her mother and the others.
When your car comes, you and I go to Moscow. Agreed?

MITIA. There has to be a search.

KOTOV. You can search all night if you want to – as long as
we're gone by the time they come back tomorrow. You get
me to Moscow as soon as possible, pretty boy. Does the
number 2315 mean anything to you, Dmitri Andreevich?

MITIA. I think I can guess.

KOTOV. No, you can't. It's Comrade Stalin's direct line. And
when I ring it tonight, dear boy, you will be sitting in such a
big pile of shit, you and your bosses'll be cleaning it out of
your ears for weeks.

A pause. MITIA *starts to chuckle. Then to laugh. Silence. He
sighs.*

MITIA. I don't think you understand at all, Comrade.

KOTOV. I'll be ready at four. You say nothing to anybody.

MITIA. Is that another order? I don't think you know what
you're dealing with, General.

He looks at his watch.

You have one hour left. How do you intend to spend it?

KOTOV. How do you think? By burning papers? Or hunting
out my secret cyanide capsule? You've made a big mistake,
Brother Grimm. Somebody's pulling your leg. Maybe I'll tell
them, 'We should pity him, not punish him.'

MITIA. What?

KOTOV. Hasn't it occurred to you – you've been set up here?
Can't you see what's coming? Think about it, pretty boy.
Who will dare touch me? I'm Kotov. Who will dare touch
Kotov?

MITIA *looks right into his eyes.*

MITIA. I'll repeat that to you word for word – 'Who will dare touch Kotov?' – in five or six days' time when you're crawling through your own shit to admit – in writing – that since 1920 you've been spying for the Germans, that since 1923 you've been spying for the Japanese, that you're a terrorist – and that your sole aim in life has been to murder Comrade Stalin. And if you don't sign the paper that confesses to all of that, you scum... then we will remind you that you have a wife.

Silence. KOTOV drops him to the ground with one punch in the face.

Trumpets, trombones, drums and voices are suddenly arriving into the garden. NADIA arrives, dressed for the trip to the zoo.

NADIA. Pappa, Pappa! The Pioneers are coming to see you, Pappa! The Kotov Brigade is here! Uncle Mitia, are you all right?

MITIA *simply gets to his feet and smiles.*

MITIA. Perfectly.

NADIA. I'll get your tunic, Pappa!

She dashes into the house.

MITIA. I'll give you one chance. Go now and type your confession. I take you and the confession to Moscow tonight – two big feathers in my cap – and maybe, maybe... they'll spare Maroussia... as the wife of a traitor. We all have a choice, Comrade.

KOTOV *stares at him.*

Scene Four

The PIONEERS *enter the garden and line up in front of the dacha.*

Everyone comes out of the dacha to witness the event, all dressed for an outing by now, except KIRIK *and* MOKHOVA.

A young GIRL PIONEER *salutes* KOTOV, *who stands to attention.*

NADIA *arrives with* KOTOV's *tunic and peaked hat, which he puts on. She stands beside him, saluting.*

The music stops.

GIRL PIONEER. The Pioneer detachment that proudly bears Comrade Kotov's name – glorious hero of the Revolution, renowned Bolshevik, and legendary general – has come to take an oath before the man who honours them. One, two!

PIONEERS. We young Leninist Pioneers, of the detachment bearing the name of the legendary General Kotov –

KOTOV *sees that* NADIA's *salute is askew. He corrects it.*

Everybody is standing to attention and saluting.

Only MITIA *is uninvolved. He comes and stands beside* MAROUSSIA *at the balustrade. He looks at her face. She looks into his eyes and walks into the garden and stands right beside* KOTOV. *She salutes him too.*

– hero of the Civil War, faithful disciple and brother-in-arms of Comrade Stalin, renowned Bolshevik, decorated many times, before all our comrades, and in the presence of Comrade Kotov, solemnly swear to be the faithful upholders of the Great Cause of Lenin, Stalin, and the heroes of the Great Revolution!

The PIONEERS *salute* KOTOV. *The trumpets play, the band plays, the* PIONEERS *march away, and everyone goes back inside.*

LIDIA. Let's get going to the zoo!

ELENA. Nadia! Nadia!

But NADIA *stands silently with her mother, saluting* KOTOV, *and he them, while* MITIA *watches from the verandah. He saunters indoors.* KOTOV *picks up* NADIA.

KOTOV. Nadia. A promise is a promise. But I can't come to the zoo today.

She's about to protest.

Wait, wait. You can go with Mamma. Sit on her knee in the front. Uncle Vsevolod will drive. The grannies in the back.

NADIA. Can I drive a little way?

KOTOV. Ask Vsevolod Konstantinovich.

NADIA. But I have your permission, General?

KOTOV. You have my permission. Nadia, listen to me. I have to work with Uncle Mitia tonight. A big car is coming. Keep a look out, will you? If you see the big car, come and get me. Don't speak to anybody. Just come and get me. Not a word. Promise?

NADIA. Promise.

She salutes. He salutes. He goes in. She sits on the verandah and waits.

Scene Five

The lights change as the afternoon wears on.

Enter three NKVD OFFICERS. *They walk slowly, not sure of their bearings. They are all heavy-set men, all wearing raincoats and hats, despite the warmth of the day. They see* NADIA *sitting on the steps of the verandah.*

BLOKHIN. Is this dacha number 9?

She nods. She points to a big sign saying '9'.

Where is everybody?

She holds out her hands to say 'Who knows?'

They decide to wait. They move up onto the verandah and unwrap their lunches. They eat with their fingers. Pickles, dips, crackers, flasks of tea. She sits with them at the table.

NADIA. I'm not supposed to talk to you.

BLOKHIN *nods.*

Are you the men from the big car?

BLOKHIN. Uh-huh.

NADIA. I've been expecting you.

BLOKHIN (*worried*). Uh-huh?

NADIA. Are you looking for Uncle Mitia?

MIRONOV. It's his niece...?

NADIA. Not really. I just call him that.

BLOKHIN. It's the right place.

MIRONOV. Is this his daughter, you think?

BLOKHIN. Could be.

Silence. They eat. She focuses on the third officer, ARONIN.

NADIA. Hello.

ARONIN. Hello.

NADIA. We're going to the zoo.

ARONIN. Uh-huh?

NADIA. I'm going to drive the car.

ARONIN. That's nice.

NADIA. We drive through the fields.

MIRONOV. Lot to say for herself, hasn't she…?

NADIA. What's that you're eating?

BLOKHIN. My lunch.

NADIA. It looks nasty. Wouldn't you like some of Granny's cake?

The OFFICERS *react oddly to this.*

BLOKHIN. No. Thank you.

OLGA (*offstage*). Nadia…?

NADIA. Grandma.

She dashes indoors.

MIRONOV. Bold, isn't she?

BLOKHIN. Well trained as well. One mouthful of 'Granny's cake' and…

He mimes death. They nod. Silence.

Have you seen him before?

MIRONOV. In the flesh? No. Only on posters.

ARONIN. I saw him on a newsreel.

They slurp their tea. MITIA *arrives, angry with them.*

MITIA. Get up. Get over there. Who said you could sit here?

They move smartly and stand in the garden. Enter
MAROUSSIA.

MAROUSSIA. What is this work you and Serguei have to do?
Do the police need his help with something? He promised
Nadia a trip to the zoo.

MITIA. You'll still go to the zoo. All except Serguei Petrovich.

MAROUSSIA. But what work? Who are these men? Hello.

They doff their hats.

MITIA. I don't know anything about work. My colleagues are
driving me back to Moscow and Serguei Petrovich asked for
a lift.

MAROUSSIA. But he could come with us.

MITIA *shrugs.*

Are you leaving now?

MITIA. Soon.

MAROUSSIA. Mitia. Will you come back here again...?

A pause.

MITIA. No.

A pause.

MAROUSSIA. You never said why you came.

A pause.

MITIA. One day, many years ago, I was at your father's
bedside. He was already very ill; he wasn't always coherent
by the end. But suddenly he opened his eyes wide, took my
hand, and said to me: 'It's annoying, Mitia. I've had such a
long, fascinating, beautiful life in this extraordinary land.
And what do I see before dying? Geese on trains. Geese on
trains. How very... very... stupid... and annoying.' I found
out later those were his last words.

MAROUSSIA. I didn't know.

MITIA. There are many things you will never know, Maroussia. Many things nobody will tell you.

A pause.

MAROUSSIA. There are some things I never told you, Mitia. Goodbye.

MITIA. Goodbye, Marousse.

She goes inside, as ELENA, LIDIA *and* OLGA *emerge, ready for the trip.*

VSEVOLOD. My name's Vsevolod Konstantinovich.

BLOKHIN. Uh-huh?

VSEVOLOD. You're colleagues of Dmitri Andreevich?

BLOKHIN. Uh-huh.

VSEVOLOD. Forgive my curiosity, but... colleagues from where exactly...?

BLOKHIN. From the Philharmonic, can't you tell?

VSEVOLOD. The Philharmonic! He never said a word!

The OFFICERS *starts humming a folk tune together. They are smirking.*

Olga, what do you think of that? Mitia pretends to us that he plays the piano in a restaurant when in fact he plays in the Philharmonic!

LIDIA. The Philharmonic!? Mitia, why not invite your friends inside? We could sing together.

MITIA. There's no time. The animals will all be asleep.

ELENA. But we haven't sung together, Mitia. Like the old days. When will we get another chance? There's time, isn't there? A glass of brandy and a song.

BLOKHIN. No brandy.

OLGA. Come. Come inside.

They usher the OFFICERS *inside.* OLGA *takes* MITIA *by the hand and leads him in. Soon we hear him playing the Finale of Act One of* Madame Butterfly, *the lovers eager to consummate.*

Meanwhile, KOTOV *comes out in shirt and trousers, carrying his boots, hat and tunic – covered in medals. He pulls on his boots.*

He pours a glass of vodka. NADIA *joins him.*

NADIA. So there you are. Uncle Mitia and Elena are singing.

KOTOV. Yes.

NADIA. Now we'll never get to the zoo.

KOTOV. You'll be leaving very soon.

NADIA. Have you been drinking?

KOTOV. Me?

NADIA. Yes.

He nods his head enthusiastically.

KOTOV. Yes.

NADIA. On an empty stomach.

MAROUSSIA *comes out.*

MAROUSSIA. They're singing. It's like the old times.

NADIA. He's been drinking.

MAROUSSIA. Yes. I'll have another one.

He's delighted. He pours them drinks. They toast.

KOTOV. To old times.

MAROUSSIA. Old times.

They drink.

Why are you wearing your uniform?

KOTOV. Official business.

MAROUSSIA. With all your medals…?

KOTOV. Better on my chest than on top of a pine box.

NADIA. We better get him ready, Mamma.

They dress him in his tunic. He lifts up NADIA *and puts his arm around* MAROUSSIA*'s waist. They listen to the singing.*

KOTOV. You're not angry with me, are you? Either of you?

MAROUSSIA. For what?

KOTOV. For not coming to the zoo.

MAROUSSIA. No. I'm not angry with you. How could we be angry with you?

She puts her hand on his shoulder. NADIA *kisses him.*

The music ends in applause and everybody comes out, including MOKHOVA, *also dressed for the trip.*

The OFFICERS *are taken aback at first to walk into the living, breathing* KOTOV – *especially now he has his hat on.*

He shakes hands with each of them as they pass.

KOTOV. Kotov. Kotov. Kotov.

They each salute and pass into the garden.

MITIA. Time you were going. The animals –

OLGA. – will all be asleep. But we haven't heard your colleagues singing.

VSEVOLOD. Yes. I have an idea. How about this?

He sings, rather feebly.

(*Singing.*)
    Where are you now…?

Too high.

(*Starting again.*)
>Where are you now…?
>Where are you now,
>Spring days of love…?

Join in, gentlemen. 'Tender dreams, sweet dreams of spring…'

The OFFICERS *are just staring at him. Silence.*

BLOKHIN. We don't know it.

LIDIA has a better idea.

LIDIA. 'Evening Bells'!

ELENA/OLGA. 'Evening Bells'! Everybody knows 'Evening Bells'!

VSEVOLOD. Do you know 'Evening Bells'?

They nod, glumly. VSEVOLOD, MOKHOVA, OLGA *and the* GRANNIES *line up with the* OFFICERS.

OLGA. Mitia, you have to be Boris Konstantinovich! Give us an 'A'.

NADIA. 'Evening Bells', Pappa.

She dashes over and joins them.

MITIA. I really don't think there's –

KOTOV. There's time.

MITIA *reluctantly takes his place as the conductor of the choir. He raises his hands for silence. He gives an 'A'.*

CHOIR (*singing*).
>Those evening bells, those evening bells!
>How many a tale their music tells,
>Of youth, and home, and that sweet time,
>When last I heard their soothing chime.

They hum the next bit in harmony. KOTOV *is holding* MAROUSSIA *tight.*

MAROUSSIA. Serguei. What's wrong? Why aren't you coming to the zoo?

KOTOV. Nothing's wrong.

MAROUSSIA. You would tell me if there were…?

KOTOV. Of course. Nothing is wrong. Everything will be for the best. Have faith.

MAROUSSIA. You would never leave me without a word, would you?

KOTOV. No. I love you, Marousse.

He kisses her. She waves them all towards the road. They sing gently as they go.

CHOIR (*singing*).
>   And so 'twill be when I am gone;
>   That tuneful peal will still ring on,
>   While other bards shall walk these dells,
>   And sing your praise, sweet evening bells.

KOTOV. Get them moving along, eh? The animals… will all be asleep.

The OFFICERS fall silent. They turn towards KOTOV. MAROUSSIA looks at KOTOV and then at MITIA. And finally she understands what is happening. KOTOV shakes his head. He looks at NADIA. MAROUSSIA nods.

NADIA (*to BLOKHIN*). Were you ever at the zoo?

BLOKHIN. Uh-huh.

NADIA. Why did you leave – didn't they feed you properly?

A pause. MITIA laughs.

KOTOV. Nadia. Don't be cheeky to grown-ups…

MAROUSSIA. Come on, Nadia.

She salutes MITIA, who salutes back. She salutes KOTOV, who salutes her back. MAROUSSIA kisses KOTOV tenderly. She goes, holding NADIA's *hand. Silence. We hear a car engine start. Doors slamming. The car leaves. Silence. Then suddenly,* KIRIK *bursts onto the scene on his bike, ringing his bell.* MIRONOV *pulls a gun, but* MITIA *waves it away.* KIRIK *was unaware.*

KIRIK. Well. I'll be late for work again.

Nobody replies.

Au revoir, mes enfants!

He rides off.

Scene Six

The OFFICERS *draw their pistols as* MITIA *lights a cigarette.*

BLOKHIN. Is he armed?

MITIA *ignores the question, turning his back on the action.*

Do you carry a pistol?

KOTOV. Are you stupid? I'm a general. Of course I carry a pistol.

They point their guns at him. He takes his own from his shoulder holster and puts it on the table.

Careful, pretty boy. It's loaded.

MIRONOV *takes the pistol.*

MITIA. Start the search. No hurry. We've got all night if necessary. He's burnt everything anyway.

ARONIN *goes inside where we can see him taking books from shelves, looking in drawers, etc. He's rough and careless.* KOTOV *reaches into his tunic, which causes pistols to be pointed at him again. He pulls out a hip flask.*

BLOKHIN. Give me that.

KOTOV. What – you think I'm going to poison myself? Not a chance. I've had all day to do that. Haven't I, Mitia?

BLOKHIN. He knew we were coming?

KOTOV. Do I look stupid?

ARONIN *comes out carrying a large framed photograph of* KOTOV *and Stalin together.*

ARONIN. Look. It's him... and Comrade Stalin.

MITIA *toasts the photo of* KOTOV *and Stalin.*

KOTOV. Don't let it make you nervous. Another drink, Mitia?

MITIA *shakes his head.*

Drop of cognac, Comrade?

MIRONOV. I don't drink and I don't smoke.

KOTOV. But you talk. I was beginning to wonder.

He sips.

Well, youngsters, have we all enjoyed the celebrations of Comrade Stalin's airships and balloons? Here's to them!

He sips again. MITIA *gently takes the flask from him and pockets it. He takes* KOTOV's *pistol from* MIRONOV *and pockets that too.*

Looking at the sky, I'd say tomorrow will be a fine day. Why don't you save your friend all this wasted effort and let's get on the road? I'll take us all to a good restaurant in Moscow – my treat – we'll all have a good night's sleep – your last for a while, I would think – and in the morning I'll call Comrade Stalin. What do you say? Mm? Yes? No? 2315.

MITIA. Geese on trains.

KOTOV. What's that?

MITIA. I said: Geese on trains.

KOTOV *stands up to reach for the vodka and* BLOKHIN
pushes him roughly back into his seat. KOTOV *responds by
trying again.* BLOKHIN *smashes the butt of his pistol into*
KOTOV*'s face, cutting open his eyebrow.* MIRONOV *tries
pinning his arms, but* KOTOV *lands heavy punches on them
both. He gets a lot in return.* ARONIN *joins in and* KOTOV
*is soon beaten. His face is very bloody. They handcuff his
hands behind his head.*

He has an office at the back. Turn it over.

The OFFICERS *go. Silence.*

KOTOV. Please tell me, Mitia. Tell me…

MITIA. Tell you what?

KOTOV. Tell me what it's like to lose all the time.

MITIA. Who's losing, Sergeui?

KOTOV. You told me. You lost the war. You lost the good life.
You lost Maroussia. You became a sad man. Lonely, eh? Sad.
Life didn't raise you up as you thought it should.

MITIA. Those who fly too high get burnt by the sun.

KOTOV. That can be true, Comrade. But at least I know who
and what I am. Here. Inside. I'm sure.

MITIA. This time next week you won't be so sure.

KOTOV. And who will you be next week, Mitia? Doctor?
Summer Santa? Blind beggar? Piano player? Tap dancer?
Whore? Which Mitia will turn up for work next week? You
don't know, Mitia. Because you're nothing. You're empty.
You're just somebody who wanted an easy life.

MITIA. I wanted meaning. You took away meaning, you and
your friends, and gave us undeniable truth in its place. I
wanted life's journey. You gave us a fixed destination. Mine
the same as everybody else's.

KOTOV. The same as everybody else's. How disappointing for
a special little boy like Mitia. And now he has nothing left to
live for – except revenge.

MITIA. No, Comrade General. I will go to my grave knowing I
did my Motherland and the Party the greatest possible
service. I tore away the false mask of a terrorist and a traitor.

KOTOV. You really believe that I, Kotov, could be a German
spy…?

MITIA. It is hard to believe. But when you sign the
confession… I will reluctantly have to believe it.

KOTOV. There will be no confession, Comrade.

MITIA. Oh, there will, Comrade. Because if you hesitate to
obey us, we will have to remind you… that you have a
daughter.

Tears well in KOTOV'*s eyes and he has to turn aside. The*
OFFICERS *come back.* BLOKHIN *signals: 'Nothing.'*

I was too late. He just admitted he was tipped off. He
destroyed all his letters.

DRIVER (*offstage*). Hello? Hello? Anybody home?

Enter the DRIVER, *hoping to find* MOKHOVA. *The*
OFFICERS *subtly move to surround him.*

Oh. I was looking for the maid. Her name is Mokhova. I
think.

MITIA. She's gone to the zoo. Who are you? You were here
earlier. And at the river. Asking questions.

DRIVER. I've been looking all day for Zagorienko. Or
Zagorienka.

BLOKHIN. Never heard of either.

DRIVER. No. They don't exist. I've covered every inch of road
between here and Moscow. I made a mistake. All I found
was balloons. Now I've run out of petrol.

BLOKHIN. Balloons?

DRIVER. Airships. In the middle of the forest – would you
believe it? – I came across a huge clearing. A hundred men –

more. And they're building the biggest balloon you ever saw in your life. Scaffold a hundred feet high. Were they angry when they saw me! 'Get out of here, you moron! We'll snap your head off your shoulders, you peasant!' You could tell they were angry. They weren't interested in Zagorienko. Or Zagorienka.

Silence. They're not sure what to do with him. He realises he's in the middle of something he shouldn't be seeing.

I'm... I'm just an ordinary Joe. I just got lost, that's all.

Silence.

MITIA. Get out of here.

DRIVER. Thank you.

He starts to go, but catches sight of KOTOV in profile and is struck dumb. He steps forward to see him more clearly.

It is. Kotov? Is it really Kotov?

MITIA. No. It's just somebody who used to look like him.

The DRIVER steps near enough to see clearly.

DRIVER. It is. It's Comrade Kotov! What happened to his face?

Too late, he realises he's in serious trouble as they pull him away.

BLOKHIN. Papers?

DRIVER. I'll go. You'll never see me again.

BLOKHIN. With no petrol?

DRIVER. I didn't see anything. It isn't Kotov. I made a mistake. I'll walk home.

BLOKHIN. But you're lost, Comrade. Papers.

He hands over his papers. KOTOV turns back towards them. He starts to cry. It becomes a cry of misery. The DRIVER stares at him and decides to run for it.

MITIA. Halt.

He puts up his hands and turns round.

DRIVER. The address faded away, Comrade. Zagorienko. I'm a
poor man. I have no money to offer. I have no wife. Just two
kids who need a mother. I thought... Mokhova... My papers
are all in order. I thought it was Kotov, but now I can see it
isn't. It's nothing like Kotov. I'll just go.

MITIA. Be quiet.

He is silent. MITIA *goes to* KOTOV.

Can you see? Can you hear? You're nothing like Kotov.

*He stands thinking. He takes a cigarette from his case. He
lights a match. Just then he sees a giant balloon rising into
the sky above the forest, carrying a huge portrait of Stalin.*
MITIA *slowly draws himself to attention and salutes. He
smiles. They all look at it.*

DRIVER. Comrade Stalin.

MITIA. Burn his papers. And his driving licence. We're
leaving. Clear up this mess.

He indicates the DRIVER. BLOKHIN *shoots him dead.*

Bring him to the car. Wait there for me.

They pull KOTOV *to his feet.* KOTOV *and* MITIA *look into
each other's eyes.*

KOTOV. What has become of us...?

The OFFICERS *take* KOTOV *away.* MITIA *takes* KOTOV's
*pistol from his pocket. He removes all six bullets. He
replaces one of them. He pours a vodka. He knocks it back.
He puts the gun to his head. After a struggle, he pulls the
trigger. A blank. He puts down the gun. He pours and drinks
another vodka. He puts the gun to his head. Another
desperate struggle. He pulls the trigger. A blank. He puts
down the gun. His hand reaches for the vodka bottle. He
stops. He picks up the pistol, puts it quickly to his head and
pulls the trigger immediately. As the shot is fired...*

Blackout.

Then the following is projected onto the giant portrait of Stalin:

'Kotov, Serguei Petrovich, Commander of the Red Army, was shot on 12 October 1936. He was posthumously rehabilitated on 27 November 1956.'

'Kotova, Maroussia Borisovna, was sentenced to ten years in a prison camp and died there in 1940. She was posthumously rehabilitated on 27 November 1956.'

'Nadia Kotova was arrested with her mother on 12 August 1936 and fully rehabilitated on 27 November 1956. She lives in retirement in Kazakhstan, where she worked as a music teacher.'

The End.